THE LAST YEARS

THE LAST YEARS

CAROLINE REHDER

Copyright © 2020 Caroline Rehder

The moral right of the author has been asserted.

Apart from any fair dealing for the purposes of research or private study, or criticism or review, as permitted under the Copyright, Designs and Patents Act 1988, this publication may only be reproduced, stored or transmitted, in any form or by any means, with the prior permission in writing of the publishers, or in the case of reprographic reproduction in accordance with the terms of licences issued by the Copyright Licensing Agency. Enquiries concerning reproduction outside those terms should be sent to the publishers.

Matador
9 Priory Business Park,
Wistow Road, Kibworth Beauchamp,
Leicestershire. LE8 0RX
Tel: 0116 279 2299
Email: books@troubador.co.uk
Web: www.troubador.co.uk/matador
Twitter: @matadorbooks

ISBN 978 1838590 482

British Library Cataloguing in Publication Data.
A catalogue record for this book is available from the British Library.

Printed and bound by CPI Group (UK) Ltd, Croydon, CR0 4YY
Typeset in 11pt Sabon MT by Troubador Publishing Ltd, Leicester, UK

Matador is an imprint of Troubador Publishing Ltd

For Robert

CONTENTS

THE LAST DANCE	1
MOUSE THE UNREADY	95

THE LAST DANCE

Hercules	in his sixties, recently widowed
Hecuba	the ghost of his wife
Cat	the family cat
Dog	the family dog

(Hercules is trying to reconcile himself to the loss of his wife who has died three days earlier. There is a circle of light on the stage. Hecuba moves in and out of this light. Sometimes she is clearly visible, at other times she is a shadowy figure. Hecuba is lying propped up against the wall, Hercules is trying to lift her off the floor and into an armchair. Cat and Dog are watching. Dog always takes things seriously, Cat is sharp and sarcastic.)

Hercules: Well, don't just stand there!

(They all three help Hecuba into the chair.)

Dog: Sit!

Hecuba *(Wobbles.)*

Stay!

(Hercules goes to his desk to try to sort through papers.)

Hecuba *(Wobbles.)*

Stay!

(Hercules finds a newspaper. He tries to read it. Dog looks over his shoulder, then removes the paper and puts it the right way

round, then removes the paper altogether and Hercules goes on reading moving his head from left to right. He is not seeing anything, doesn't notice when Dog waves a paw in front of his face. Dog folds the newspaper and adds it to a pile of newspapers.)

At fifty five pence a paper that's two thousand pence a year going to waste.

Cat: At fifty five pence a paper it's two thousand and seventy pence a year. I like to be accurate.

(Dog sniffs the air around Hercules. He pulls a face.)

Dog: Hasn't changed his clothes since it happened.

(Dog sniffs around Hecuba and pulls a face.)

Nor's she.

(Dog sprays them both with air freshener, finds the canister is empty and tosses it onto a pile of empty canisters.)

Cat: Another fortune down the drain.

(Hercules is anxiously arranging papers at his desk.)

Hecuba: *(Gets up.)*

Cat: Wait for it!

Hecuba: *(Moves noisily.)*

Cat: Warned you. Right on cue. *(to Hercules)* You want my advice, sir? Take no notice.

Hecuba: Moves closer to Hercules.

Hercules: Oh mighty Hecuba, douce queen of the night, let me think!

Cat: *(sotto voce)* You'll be lucky!

(All is quiet.)

Hecuba: *(Rustles her clothes.)*

(Hercules shakes his head as if to get rid of a fly, Dog gets a flywhisk and flourishes it, but Cat takes it off him.)

Cat: It's not a mosquito, it's HER!

Hecuba: Makes a small noise.

Hercules: OK. OK … I know. I have the funeral to arrange, family to notify, the flowers, the will—

(Hercules wants to make notes but can't decide which hand he writes with. Dog puts the pen into Hercules' right hand, but Hercules can't concentrate. He makes a gesture to indicate the area around him and pushes Hecuba out of it.)

MY space. MY chair. MY rules.

(Hercules picks up a pen, waits for Hecuba to interrupt, then starts to write notes. All is quiet.)

Cat: *(sotto voce)* Won't last.

Hecuba: *(Makes a noise.)*

Cat: Warned you.

(Hercules thumps his hand on the table in exasperation.)

The woman's restless tonight.

Hercules: Every night.

Cat: Wait for it.

Hecuba: *(Taps her foot.)*

(Hercules is suddenly dramatically sad, bent over, broken.)

Cat: There! Hercules concedes. We're in trouble again. I make that five nil to Hecuba.

Dog: *(virtuously)* We're not keeping score.

Cat: I am.

Dog: *(checking his watch)* That's more than twenty four hours she's been on the rampage. Madame's upping her game.

Cat: Never a dull moment since the day she died.

Dog: *(low voice)* Passed.

Hecuba: *(Makes a noise to get Hercules' attention.)*

(Hercules makes obeisance to her.)

Hercules: Mighty sorceress, peace.

Cat: Peace? Hecuba? Doesn't know the meaning of the word.

Hercules: It's nearly midnight—

Cat: *(hollowly)* The witching hour—

Hercules: It's been a long day—

Hercules: *(in unison)* We beg for rest.

Cat: *(in unison)* We beg for rest.

Dog: *(in unison)* We beg for rest.

Hecuba: *(Beckons Hercules sexily.)*

Cat: Hecuba!

Hecuba: *(Turns to look at Cat.)*

Cat: No flirting!

Hecuba: *(Is demure.)*

Dog: Three days we've been shut up here with nothing happening. There's stuff to be done. What's he waiting for?

Cat: *(shrugging)* Who knows!

Dog: I mean technically she's a corpse, isn't she? Why doesn't he bury her?

Cat: Praying for a miracle maybe?

Dog: Eh?

Cat: Kidding himself this is a dream he's going to wake up from?

Dog: Ah! Can't face the future without her, you mean?

Cat: Something like that.

Hecuba: *(Moves slightly flirtatiously.)*

(Hercules watches her anxiously.)

Dog: Still likes to keep him guessing!

Cat: Yup. Up to every trick in the book is our Hecuba! Miles on her broomstick last night. All around the house. Didn't leave him alone for a minute. Gave a great show, the girl she was at twenty when they met, the woman at forty, at sixty. Poor stupid fellow didn't know whether he was on his head or his heels, didn't get a wink of sleep—

Dog: I know, I heard him. He was moaning and groaning all night. Enough to wake the dead. *(breaks off embarrassed, to Hecuba)* Sorry. *(to Cat)* He's lost three kilos since she – absconded—

Cat: Three kilos and three hundred grams. And she didn't abscond, she died. *(mimes dying)*

Dog: OK, since she ... you know ... maybe we could try talking to him?

Cat: If he's not listening? Waste of time.

(They're glum together.)

Not listening, not sleeping, starving himself, not doing a stroke of work, the house is a tip. I'd say desperate measures are called for.

Dog: Like what?

Cat: No idea. You?

(They think. Dog puts up a hand.)

Well?

Dog: A plumbing problem?

Cat: What kind of plumbing problem? ... Well?

Dog: *(thinking)* I'm thinking.

Cat: Well, hurry up thinking.

Dog: Don't rush me. You always rush me. Wait! Wait! ... OK, got it! A pipe bursts – *(waving a spanner)* – thanks to our ingenuity – water overflows, and drips from upstairs through the ceiling into the room below. That means right here. The ceiling is at risk, the carpet is sodden, the water level is rising, our hero is forced—

Cat: *(very sceptically)* Who?

Dog: Hercules! Our hero! Is forced into action by wet feet, surfaces from whatever dark lagoon he's currently hanging out in, fixes the pipe and la voila, finds himself back on track for coping with the demands of every day and functioning more or less normally ... what do you say?

Cat: Hmm—

Dog: It's not foolproof, but—

Cat: *(in unison)* It's worth a try.

Dog: *(in unison)* It's worth a try.

(They get two pieces of pipe that are screwed together, unscrew them, and mime getting wet as the water overflows. There is the sound of dripping. Hercules takes no notice until his feet start to get wet, he doesn't move from his chair, but takes off his shoes and socks and rolls up his trousers as if to paddle.)

Cat: Idiot, this isn't the seaside!

(Hercules shifts his chair.)

Dog: Moving to higher ground.

(Hercules looks out shielding his eyes.)

Waiting for the lifeboat.

(Hercules worried, starts to pray.)

Resigned to his fate and making his peace with the Almighty.

(Cat connects the pipe again crossly.)

Cat: *(tartly)* My guess is he's beyond help.

Dog: *(piously)* Nobody's beyond help.

Cat: Dog!

(Dog salutes.)

None of your claptrap. Remember we're on oath here to tell the truth. His wits are wandering, yes or no?

Dog: Yes.

Cat: And all because of that wretched woman!

Dog: Come on, you like Hecuba.

Cat: Not when she HAUNTS him, I don't. And she's been haunting him since the day she died.

Dog: *(sotto voce)* Passed.

Cat: She nags him from sun up to sun down, plus all through the night. It's not like her, she's an independent woman with a mind of her own, I don't see why's she bothering him like this!

Dog: Maybe she's lonely?

Cat: Yeah, well, we're all lonely! Look at him. You ever seen him so down in the dumps? We threaten him with serious water damage to the house and he can't be bothered either to call a plumber or to fix it himself. My bet is she's put a spell on him.

Dog: *(not understanding)* Eh?

Cat: HE'S FORGETTING TO EAT. What does that tell you!

Dog: He's not hungry?

Cat: It's HER doing! *(mimicking Hecuba doing a magic spell)* SHE dies – nobody asks her to, but she goes ahead anyway – and HE's punished for it. He didn't go running around after her every time she lifted her little finger when she was alive, why now?

Dog: *(hesitantly)* … guilt maybe?

Cat: *(angrily)* Guilt! It's always guilt with you … can't you think of anything else!

Dog: No.

Cat: They're man and wife for forty years and, suddenly, out of the blue, three days ago, she waits for him to leave the house on an errand and then she quits on him without a word of warning, drops down dead. He was no way prepared. Didn't see it coming. In fact was busy planning their next holiday. So now he's trying to make believe that her death is not for real and there's some way – if he's smart – he can get round it. Well good luck on that. That's when he's not beating himself up for not saying sorry for all the things that went wrong between them. If he'd really wanted to say sorry he should have taken the time to do it BEFORE she died. But no, he forgets, puts it off, doesn't have the courage, can't make the effort, she dies and he's caught with all his apologies on the tip of his tongue and it's TOO LATE. He's missed his chance to ask for forgiveness and he won't get another one. Incompetent fool! Now the two of them are messing up their final days together all for the want of a little forethought. (pointing to Hecuba) What are we left with? A wretched unsatisfied ghost in the house.

(Hercules puts up his hand.)

Make that two wretched, unsatisfied ghosts.

Dog: *(piously)* Time softens the pain. So they say.

Cat: Yeah, well, that's fine if you've GOT time. He doesn't.

Dog: He's not that old.

Cat: He's near retirement age. He could drop dead tomorrow!

Dog: Don't be cross.

Cat: I feel cross. I tell you, he's behaving like a fool. Not washing, not eating, not sleeping. It makes me nervous.

Dog: He's better than he was yesterday.

Cat: No he's not.

Dog: He cooked himself an egg for breakfast.

Cat: Didn't eat it.

Dog: And put jam on his toast.

Cat: Without removing the mould.

Dog: But these could be the first green shoots of his … er, rehabilitation.

Hecuba: *(Is moving away.)*

Hercules: *(shouting at Hecuba)* Don't you wander off!

Hecuba: *(Moves further away.)*

Hercules: I'M TALKING TO YOU, WOMAN.

(Dog and Cat cover their ears.)

Get back here! There are important matters to discuss.

Cat: You've had forty years to discuss important matters. I repeat, it is now TOO LATE!

Hecuba: *(Is moving out of the light.)*

Hercules: *(to Hecuba)* You are not going anywhere.

Hecuba: *(Stares at him haughtily.)*

Hercules: *(angrily)* What's the matter with you! Why won't you talk to me? Bitch.

Cat: *(sharply)* Hey, mind your manners.

Hercules: *(childishly)* Yeah, well, she can't just quit. I RELY on her. She knows that and she walks away. How am I going to manage without her? I'm not. Come on, you've got all the answers, tell me!

Cat: *(tiredly)* Maybe she's expecting you to use your initiative.

Hercules: What initiative?

Cat: *(very drily)* Good question!

Hercules: *(to Hecuba sulkily)* I'll wreck the place if you leave.

Cat: Here we go! Back to the nursery.

Hercules: Smash it up! See how you like that!

Hecuba: *(Shrugs.)*

Hercules: *(angrily)* What have I done? *(then suddenly defeated)* What have I not done! *(soberly)* What have I not done!

Cat: Please, take your thumb out of your mouth and stop whining.

(Hercules pouts.)

OK, I understand you want to make a dramatic gesture. My suggestion? Get her decently buried and then you throw yourself on to her grave. It's very romantic and socially more acceptable than sulking. Try it. Here's the grave. *(taking a chair)* This here's the headstone. *(acting this)* "Ah, my beloved," then you let yourself fall.

(Hercules throws himself very awkwardly on to the grave, he can't do it properly. Cat, Dog and Hecuba laugh at him.)

Not like that! Gracefully!

Hercules: *(not able to get up)* It's my arthritis. Well don't just stand there!

(Dog and Cat help him up. Once up Hercules hits out at them.)

	Stop laughing! *(turning to Hecuba)* That goes for you too! Traitor!
Cat:	Calling her names is not going to help.
Hercules:	*(mumbling angrily)* Traitor. Deserter.
Cat:	Word of advice, son. You two need to be on good terms. Now more than ever. Insulting her is not the answer.
Hercules:	*(sniffling pathetically)* I miss her. I want her back.
Dog:	*(to Cat)* You can't help feeling sorry for him. If she'd died thirty years ago when he was reasonably good looking and had a decent head of hair, he'd have looked the part for a tragedy and maybe gotten a little sympathy, now he's just one more sad old guy whose wife has died – what can you expect at that age – and hardly worth a second thought.
Hercules:	Old?
Cat:	Old!
Dog:	Who hasn't washed his face or showered in three days.

Hercules: Hmm?

Dog: *(holding his nose)* Or changed his clothes.

(a slight pause)

Hercules: *(not fully focussed, confused)* ... she's left me ...

Cat: She hasn't left exactly—

Dog: *(interrupting)* Turned up her toes.

Cat: DIED!

Hercules: No! ... no.

Dog: Three days ago you went out, remember? You came back and found her lying on the floor. You're in shock. You should take things easy.

Cat: Rubbish. You need to be busy. Not paralysed by grief. What use is that? And lucky for you, we're right here ready to get you up and running again.

Dog: First off you need a proper meal.

Hercules: I'm not hungry.

Cat: Nobody cares if you're hungry or not, it's your duty to eat.

Dog: And then what you need is a good night's sleep.

Hercules: I can't sleep.

Cat: Of course you can't if you sit up in your chair all night going over and over old photographs and letters.

Hercules: I've tried to sleep.

Cat: No, you haven't.

Hercules: *(pointing to Hecuba)* It's HER fault. SHE keeps me awake, prowling about in the midnight hours.

Hecuba: *(Shakes her head.)*

Hercules: Anytime I start to doze off—

Hecuba: *(Makes small noises, snapping her fingers, drumming them on a table etc.)*

Hercules: *(tapping his head, slightly mad)* See! Little noises that end up, up here! It's never over. There's not a moment of quiet. She's

	punishing me for what I did. I have to pay. I know Hecuba! That's her logic.
Cat.	She is NOT punishing you.
Hercules:	Well, she's definitely up to SOMETHING.
Hecuba:	*(Makes little noises.)*
Hercules:	There! You hear that! She IS punishing me. I'm sure of it.
Dog:	Sir –
Hercules:	*(resigned)* But don't worry about it. I owe her a few sleepless nights. I know what my responsibilities are.
Cat:	*(wearily)* OK, you want to be a martyr, fine!

(Dog approaches Cat and they whisper together. Dog gets his lead and goes up to Hercules with it.)

Dog: Walkies!

Hercules: Eh?

Dog: I haven't been out since the morning. I need a walk. To stretch my legs. Nice moonlight night, plenty of stars. You are not busy. You haven't done anything useful since Hecuba copped it, unless you count letting the sink back up. A walk in the fresh night air would do us both good.

Hercules: Sorry. Busy.

Dog: *(puzzled)* Busy?

Hercules: Can't you see! I'M MOURNING!

Dog: Mourning is not a full time occupation, it has to be fitted in around a normal daily routine. You know what the vet said.

Hercules: *(abstracted)* Hmmm?

Dog: *(offering the lead)* About my getting regular exercise. At least twenty minutes morning and night. Mourning or no mourning!

Hercules: *(snatching the lead off Dog)* You're lucky I don't strangle you with it. Now you listen to me. I am not leaving Hecuba alone in the house to go for walkies. Is that understood?

Cat: *(in unison)* Understood.

Dog: *(in unison)* Understood.

Hercules: *(mumbling grumpily)* Whatever the vet said. Stupid fellow, I never liked him.

(Cat sits on one side of the stage, Dog lies with his head on his paws, watching Hercules and heaving sighs annoyingly. Hercules turns on him angrily.)

Shut up.

Dog: I only sighed.

Hercules: Well, DON'T sigh.

(Cat and Dog turn their backs on Hercules, excluding him, he's fussed.)

Come on. Don't be angry. Please! Look, I'm on my own for the first time in over forty years. I'm doing my best –

Cat: *(aside to Dog, sarcastically)* He's doing his best.

Hercules: It's Hecuba's fault. She's mad at me. It hurts.

Cat: *(to Hecuba)* Tsk, tsk. Naughty girl.

Hercules: It's not a joke. I'm not eating properly, SHE WON'T LET ME SLEEP! *(to Hecuba)* I've said I'm sorry. I AM sorry. You need a rest. I need a rest.

Hecuba: *(Hovers near Hercules.)*

Hercules: Can't you trust me out of your sight for one minute?

(Dog confers with Cat.)

Dog: This is serious.

Cat: I know.

(Cat and Dog confer.)

(to Hercules) Look, you want Hecuba off your back, we have a solution to propose. It's very traditional. You make an offering Egyptian style. You buy important pieces of jewellery, expensive pottery, gold coins – you need to splash out on this one, beggar yourself if necessary – then you wrap her up in a winding sheet and you put her and your gifts in a beautiful sarcophogus – *(aside to Cat)* coffin to you and me – have a nice little ceremony – a river of tears if that's what you want, then you BURY her. That's what's needed. Afterwards it's tea and cake with the mourners, and after that you wave the

	mourners goodbye, and then you head back to Home Sweet Home—
Hercules:	What I head back to is an empty house! Wonderful! Love it!
Cat:	*(sarcastically)* That's right. And let the lonely fun begin.
Hercules:	*(angrily)* No!
Cat:	OK, forget the tea and cake—
Hercules:	*(pettishly)* No way I'm heading back here. I don't like this house anymore.
Cat:	Oh, what's wrong with it?
Hercules:	Everything. I'm not going to live here.
Cat:	There's no guarantee somewhere else will be better.
Hercules:	I'm expecting to forget her. This is NOT the place to do it.
Cat:	Forget her!
Hercules:	Yup. I've made up my mind. *(to Hecuba)* Sorry, and all that—

Cat: You can't forget her!

Hercules: Yes I can. I have to. I'm not living with all these pictures and memories of her haunting me all day, everyday. You said it, desperate measures are called for. She has to be cleared out and gotten rid of. (to Hecuba) Ta ta. *(waving her away)* Away! Out of my sight!

Cat: *(to Hecuba)* You don't have to listen to this rubbish. He doesn't mean it.

Hercules: Yes, I do. I intend to survive. I intend to get out of this nightmare intact. I am not losing my mind here ... ... I AM losing my mind here ... the question is, can I imagine a life without her?

Cat: Well, can you?

Hercules: No. *(to Hecuba)* You tricked me!

Hecuba: *(Shrugs.)*

Cat: Eh?

Hercules: Yes you did. You and I had an agreement about the future. A plan!

Cat: Oh? This is the first I've heard of any plan.

Hercules: Well, we did. A plan where I was going to die first and SHE was the one who was going to be left behind.

Cat: That wasn't a plan. That was a vague assumption on your part of what might happen after you'd been reading the mortality statistics.

Hercules: It WAS a plan. She agreed she was going to be there for me. I'm on my death bed, she's holding my hand, kissing my forehead, tenderly whispering good bye – in short, getting me through the whole sorry business of dying in style. We had it all programmed, but no, SHE has to ignore the programme and go first. *(to Hecuba)* You cheated!

Dog: *(seriously)* I don't think she passed away to spite you.

Cat: *(exasperated)* Died!

Hercules: What do you know!

Cat: *(airily)* I wonder if he has any idea how stupid he sounds?

Hercules: Yes, I do, no, yes, yes. *(ashamed, but can't prevent himself from turning on Hecuba)* We had a contract.

Cat: Verbal, wouldn't hold up in court.

Hercules: *(to Hecuba)* You promised!

Hecuba: *(Shrugs.)*

Hercules: "Your honours, it was a binding agreement."

Cat: *(in unison, as a judge)* "Ummmm."

Dog: *(in unison, as a judge)* "Ummmmm.

Dog: Difficult case this."

Cat: "No it isn't, the plaintiff's a fool."

Hercules: Behave!

Dog: You behave!

Hercules: What have I done!

Dog: Nothing! I think that's what we're complaining about. We haven't had a decent meal or a walk or a proper conversation since Hecuba left—

Cat: Died.

Dog: And we're getting anxious about our long term future if you crack up.

Cat: It may not matter to you if you miss your dinner but it does to me, plus we need our sleep—

Hecuba: *(Makes a noise to attract attention.)*

Hercules: *(wearily)* What is it now? What do you WANT?

Dog: What all of us want under the circumstances. Another twenty four hours, another life, another chance, to start over, to be young again—

Hercules: *(miserably)* Don't! Please.

Dog: But this time to dazzle. To get things right, to put things right, to make amends—

Hecuba: *(Nods sadly.)*

Hercules: *(to Hecuba)* That's impossible. As you know very well. It's stupid even to think about it. Now go away and leave me alone.

Hecuba: *(Is standing and looking at Hercules angrily.)*

Hercules: What are you staring at me for? I can't give you your life back. It's cruel to keep asking … cruel, evil, stupid … miserable … bitch. *(his*

>   *voice trails off like a child who knows he's gone too far)*

Hecuba: *(Walks away in a huff.)*

Dog: Now you've done it.

Hercules: Good riddance.

Dog: And the moment she's out of sight you'll want her back.

>   *(Cat, fed up, ostentatiously curls up to go to sleep and purrs annoyingly. Hercules begins to moan.)*

>   *(to Cat)* Shhhh.

Cat: If he shushes, I'll shush.

>   *(Cat purrs noisily, Hercules is annoyed and kicks at Cat, Dog intervenes barking, Cat hisses, it's a moment of chaos. They separate and stand as far away from each other as possible, Cat and Hercules mouthing and gesturing insults. Hecuba watches. Dog is the peacemaker.)*

Dog: *(to Hecuba and Hercules)* There's something wrong here!

(Hercules and Hecuba nod like naughty children.)

Let me guess! You two had a fight?

(Hercules and Hecuba nod again.)

The day she died, before you left the house to go on your errand? You rowed? Correct?

Hercules: *(indignantly)* No.

Dog: Well, did you?

Hercules: *(low voice)* We rowed.

Dog: Thought so. And YOU started it.

Hercules: No.

Dog: *(as to a child)* You know what happens to liars? They get their mouths washed out with soap and no sweeties for a week.

Hercules: *(very low, ashamed)* I started it.

Dog: Thought so.

Hercules: I'm sorry now.

Dog: Of course you are. But now is too late. A serious row?

Hercules: No. That's the truth.

Cat: *(sotto voce)* As if you'd know the truth!

Dog: So under ordinary circumstances it would have blown over?

Hercules: Yes, leaving misery and self doubt in its wake.

Dog: If that row was less than point zero five on the Richter scale, the continental plates would hardly have budged, there would have been NO damage to life or property and I don't think it would disgrace you to forget it.

Hercules: I can't forget it.

Dog: Yes you can. You have to put it behind you. Now!

Hercules: *(shouting angrily at Hecuba)* Forgive me!

Hecuba: *(Turns away.)*

Hercules: You see that! Monster!

Cat: Perfect! Just what the mediator ordered.

Hercules: *(upset with himself)* Sorry. Sorry, sorry, sorry –

Cat: That's not going to help.

Hercules: *(half crying)* I've been punished enough.

Cat: Hankies at the ready!

Hercules: *(to Hecuba)* You know I don't mean the things I say.

Dog: *(seriously)* Yes you do.

Hercules: *(to Hecuba, tearfully)* Yes, well, it's your duty not to listen when I'm angry. I've told you often enough.

Cat: Stop snivelling.

Hercules: *(to Hecuba)* I want to make up.

Cat: You can't shout at her one minute and expect to make up the next.

Hercules: *(to Cat)* I know. I'm a fool. *(to Hecuba)* Please!

Hecuba: *(Does not respond.)*

Hercules: Don't make me beg.

Hecuba: *(Turns away.)*

Hercules: *(angrily)* Well, that's it, I'm not saying I'm sorry again.

Cat: OK, here's my suggestion. You storm upstairs to your bedroom, you slam the door, you play loud music, you shout insults through the keyhole—

Hercules: *(angrily)* Get off me!

Hecuba: *(Thinks Hercules is talking to her and takes offence.)*

Hercules: *(to Hecuba)* I was talking to Cat.

Hecuba: *(Turns away.)*

Hercules: *(genuinely upset)* I was. I promise!

Hecuba: *(Is angry.)*

Hercules: Miserable cow.

Hecuba: *(Moves to the back of the stage and is no longer clearly visible.)*

Hercules: *(in despair)* You can't just walk away … … I need you … get back here … *(holding his head as he loses the image of her)*

Cat: Some of us are trying to sleep.

(Hercules kicks at Cat who hisses back.)

Dog: *(quietly to Hercules)* My suggestion? Say sorry!

Hercules: Sorry? To Hecuba? Never.

Dog: To Cat first. You need him. Then Hecuba. A down-on-your-knees proper apology.

Hercules: For what? I'm not sorry! We were going to get old together. She was the one ratted. *(to Hecuba)* SPEAK, damn you! Open your mouth. *(singing)* "Don't leave me this way." SAY something.

Cat: *(one eye open)* Try lying her back til her eyes close.

(Hercules lies Hecuba back like a doll.)

Now lift her back up and she may say "mama."

Hercules: *(shaking Hecuba)* I'm going to MAKE her talk to me.

Cat: Oh, how?

Hercules: I'll need an electric socket, a live cable, you two can hold her down—

Cat: Hercules! Ghosts can not be tortured.

Hercules: *(grumbling)* More's the pity.

Cat: All this for one stupid little quarrel. Forget it, it's time to move on!

Hercules: *(very indignantly)* Move on!

Cat: Why not? What's the point of waiting? The clock's ticking, the minutes are slipping by, our time here is limited—

Hercules: *(not listening to Cat, angrily to Hecuba)* Why won't you speak to me? What have I done? *(in despair, quietly)* What have I not done? What mistakes haven't I made? What petty grievances haven't I harboured? Let's count the grudges, the fights I picked for no good reason, the promises I made and broke... you HAVE counted, haven't you? You've added them all up and said "That's it. Enough. I'll take revenge."

Dog: *(sadly)* Stop! This is all your imagination.

Hercules: *(seriously to Hecuba)* I know I failed you but it was your fault too. You expected too much. I could never live up to whatever your dreams were. I was frightened you'd leave, find someone better.

Dog: *(whispering to Cat)* What he's trying to say is that he was jealous.

Cat: You were jealous?

Hercules: Of course not.

Cat: Go on, spit it out, own up.

Hercules: OK, I was jealous, clumsy—

Cat: Crazy more like!

Hercules: I couldn't help myself.

Hecuba: *(Acts flirtatiously.)*

Hercules: See!

Cat: See what?

Hercules She's doing it on purpose.

Cat: Well, if you're going to be jealous for no good reason what do you expect?

Hecuba: *(Is flirtatious.)*

Cat: *(to Hecuba)* You, stop your nonsense.

Hecuba: Stops being flirtatious.

Cat: *(to Hercules)* Now let's get this straight. Are you seriously suggesting that Hecuba, alive, was unfaithful to you?

Hercules: … yes … no, no.

Cat: Well, was she or wasn't she?

Hercules: No.

Cat: Then why all the fuss?

Hercules: *(helplessly)* I don't know. I just can't stop thinking about what if she had been?

Cat: And what if she had been?

Hercules: *(coldly)* I wouldn't owe her. I could walk away.

Cat: Walk away?

Hercules: I'd be free. No obligations. She'd be rotting in hell owing ME. Instead of the other way around, me rotting in hell owing HER.

Cat: Well, I categorically forbid you to pursue this line of enquiry.

Hercules: Yes sir.

Cat: It's a waste of everyone's time. You do owe her. You can't walk away. And that's final.

Hercules: Easy for you to say.

Cat: No more false accusations.

Hercules: *(rebelliously)* You don't know for certain they're false.

Cat: OK, unverifiable accusations. And NO MORE FIGHTING.

Hercules: It's Hecuba wants a fight. She stomps round the house all night so I can't get a wink of sleep, she won't let me eat, or read. And of course, she won't speak! Just LOOKS at me!

Cat: *(tartly, mimicking Hercules)* "Each glance a dagger to my heart."

Hercules: *(interested)* I was going to say a knife in my gut but maybe a dagger in my heart is better, more poetic! *(to Dog)* What do you think, a knife in the gut, or a dagger in the heart?

Dog: *(disgusted)* Me? I don't do "poetic."

Hercules: Cat?

Cat: Poetic? Moi?

Hercules: Knife or dagger? Definitely dagger! *(suddenly enthusiastic)* You know, that's given me a great idea.

Cat: *(very glumly)* Now we're for it.

Hercules: I'll write a poem for her! A long poem in praise of Hecuba! It will make me, *(correcting himself)* her, her, famous. She'd like that.

Cat: *(to Dog)* A poem? It's not ticking a lot of boxes for me. How about you?

Dog: *(very seriously, and puzzled)* I'm not sure I see the point of a poem.

Cat: There isn't one.

Dog: *(to Hercules)* Sir, I think the nos have it.

Hercules: *(reciting)* "I miss you by the fireside,
My heart is always yours.
Think not that it is over,
I'll love you evermore."

Cat: *(to Hecuba very sarcastically)* Well, if that doesn't pull at your heartstrings, nothing will!

Hecuba: *(Has her hands over ears not to hear the poem.)*

Hercules: She's dissing me again.

Dog: *(very seriously)* Not you. The poem.

Cat: *(under his breath)* Let's be accurate, you too.

Dog: Look, if you want to ease her passage into the next world with a choice offering, you stick to the bling, a nice diamond bracelet for example. I don't think poems, your poems anyway, are going to do it for her.

Hercules: *(muttering)* It was short, it rhymed, what more do you want!

Cat: *(to Hecuba)* Well, say thank you. We've saved you from having a poem by Hercules on your conscience.

Hecuba: *(Bobs a little thank you curtsey.)*

Cat: And now, please, don't diss him again.

Dog: It makes our lives a misery.

Cat: Behave or I'll find him a nice, RICH widow and together they'll rearrange the furniture, paint the walls fuchsia, turn your portrait to the wall and you'll be wiped clean off the map.

Hecuba: *(Puts up a hand to her forehead in Victorian horror.)*

Hercules: Leave her alone!

Hecuba: *(Moves slowly to exit.)*

Hercules: *(to Hecuba)* Don't listen to Cat. He has no manners. It was nothing, the trees rustling, night noises, words that flicker and die out ... the past is untouchable – it can't be changed, broken up, damaged ... no one touches your portrait while I'm alive ...

Dog: Well, don't stop, she's enjoying it.

Hercules: *(pleadingly to Hecuba)* Weren't we happy?

Cat: *(tartly)* There's no need to sound so miserable about it.

Hercules: *(to Cat in a low voice)* She was alone when she died.

Dog: I know. It's a problem. You have to give up thinking about it.

Hercules: I can't.

Dog: You must.

Hercules: Who knows what she suffered!

Cat: Water under the bridge.

Hercules: She needed me.

Cat: For God's sake, STOP TORTURING YOURSELF. What good does it do!

Hercules: She was scared of dying. (looking at Hecuba) Poor pitiful creature.

Cat: Pitiful! Hecuba!

Hercules: Pitiful! Hecuba! Yes! You don't know her like I do. The private Hecuba. The one who has night terrors, black, black moments of despair, a crushing sense of failure that comes and goes hourly some days. You choose not to notice. You close your eyes and nap through the bad times. Good for you! But bad times there are that are an agony to her and I'm there to witness them. I see it all, her suffering and misery. She doesn't spare me, goddam her.

Dog: This goes on, he'll be making himself ill.

Hercules: *(looking from one to the other)* She was never satisfied. She couldn't be. Her expectations were unreal. She wanted more. If there were moments of peace, and who knows if there were, they were random, erratic, not to be counted on. That's a damning legacy to leave.

Hecuba: *(Moves towards Hercules.)*

Cat: *(sternly to Hecuba)* Back off. Give him some air. Let him breathe. Rest in peace, goddam you!

Hecuba: *(Moves away.)*

Hercules: "Rest in Peace!" Whoever rests in peace!

Dog: Shhh.

Hecuba: *(Prowls around anxiously.)*

Hercules: Look at her. Never still.

Dog: Take no notice.

Hecuba: *(Mimes tears.)*

Dog: Turn your head the other way.

Hercules: I can't.

(Dog drags Hercules away and makes him turn his back on Hecuba.)

You could never be happy! Not deep down, through and through.

Cat: Nobody can.

Hercules: Why couldn't you be happy? Was that too much to ask? And now! Why can't you let me forget how you suffered? Why is it I have to remember? Don't I have worries enough? ... But we're in it together, right? If you suffer, I suffer. That's what we signed up to. The price of love.

Hecuba: *(Is moving towards Hercules beseechingly.)*

Cat: Leave him alone. You come one step closer and we call up the cavalry.

(Cat and Dog push Hecuba back.)

Stop hassling him and stay there or we get a court order restricting your movements.

Hecuba: *(Gives them the finger.)*

Cat: If you can't lighten up he'll shut you out for good and walk away. Be smart, don't push him so hard.

Hecuba: *(Mimes tears.)*

Cat: That's just the attitude I'm talking about. If you want this affair to last, then change your tactics. Let him look on the past without a dark shadow hanging over it. It's your regrets that are killing him.

Hecuba: *(Gestures sorrow.)*

Cat: No more tears. Give him a break. The poor silly fellow is not made of stone.

(Hercules picks up a photo and shows it to Dog.)

Hercules: That's her the day we met. Remember, I'd never planned on selling my freedom for a pretty face, I'd planned not to – no surrender, that was my motto! I was young, free, I wasn't going to let myself be tied down, I was going to live life on my own terms and to the full. But one fine day, there she is, standing in my path, the way you see her now, HYPNOTISING me. I can't take my eyes off her. *(tapping his head)* She marches in, makes herself at home. What can I do? I struggle, the fly in marmalade, I surrender. Of course I do. I'm not a fool, I know when I'm beaten.

(Hercules gets a pen and a piece of paper and starts drawing.)

(with a complete change of tone) I've made a decision. I'm going to build a mausoleum for her. Something that will stand forever, splendid, magnificent—

Dog: Eh?

Hercules: A mausoleum! As a memorial!

Dog: *(to Cat)* I see trouble ahead.

Hercules: *(showing it to Dog and Cat)* Here's a sketch.

Dog: *(whispering to Cat)* I know it's awful but it's better than the poem.

Cat: No it's not.

Hercules: Well?

(Cat and Dog study the sketch, hold it upside down etc, mystified.)

Cat: I think for once, Dog's right, it's awful.

Dog: *(interrupting quickly, in a posh voice, mother to child)* "It's lovely, darling."

Hercules: *(admiring it)* See what I do here?

(Cat snatches the paper off Hercules and tears it up. Hercules' face puckers.)

Dog: "It IS lovely darling, but it would cost billions we don't have to build."

Cat: It's not lovely. Plus it wouldn't stand up.

Dog: *(whispering)* Well, PRETEND it's lovely.

Cat: I can't.

Dog: What harm would it do your conscience to lie in a good cause?

Cat: I don't have a conscience but I do like to be accurate. That is a horrible mausoleum. It's horrible as a sketch and would be even worse for real. It has one saving grace, it's not as bad as the poem.

Dog: It would give him something to do.

Cat: *(grumpily)* Dog, believe me. He'd be a laughing stock if either the mausoleum or the poem ever came to the public's attention. Take my word for it. I have his best interests at heart and they are not served by letting him make a fool of himself building a mausoleum that monstrous.

Dog: It's grief clouding his judgement.

Cat: All the more reason to speed up!

Dog: Speed what up?

Cat: The mourning process. We need to get the whole sorry business over and done with, so that grief STOPS clouding his judgement and we can get back to something like normal.

Dog: We can't speed it up. Mourning has a beat of its own that can't be hurried. And remember, he'll be retiring soon, he won't have anything else but Hecuba to think about. Building a mausoleum would keep him busy. Give him something to get up in the morning for.

Cat: Don't be an idiot.

Dog: *(dreaming)* He can lay HER place for breakfast, let HER chair be sacrosanct, let HER music be playing, Her wishes be paramount, then out to the garden to put another brick in the wall. It's an option. Then maybe he can chart her family tree, give her a history—

Cat: *(shivering)* The past is over, frozen matter. Why drag himself back there?

Dog: There were sunny days.

Cat: There are sunny days in the future too. Why not consider those? *(to Hercules)* But you won't, will you? They're off limits, forbidden fruit. You're not a youngster, you don't have much time left. Why are you wasting it. And what was so special about her? Think of the times she was late with meals – late with meals! Six hours on one occasion and not a word of apology. Is that someone you put on a pedestal the moment they die? I don't think so! I say we set a date.

Dog: Eh?

Cat: We agree to put our hearts and souls into grieving for six months, nine if you prefer, and then we pull out, job done.

Dog: It's not that simple.

Cat: Yes it is.

Dog: Hercules won't want to pull out.

Cat: Too bad what Hercules wants. I'm interested in what I want! I say we set a date and stick to it.

Dog: Cat, grieving is not contract employment. We don't clock in and clock out. We work twenty four seven—

Cat: *(drily)* I've noticed!

Dog: There are no holidays. It's a labour of love that goes on for years. Even then it's a lottery whether he recovers or not. Make up your mind to it, he may never quit writing poems or designing mausoleums. It's in the lap of the gods.

Cat: *(not wanting to listen)* La, la, la, la—

Dog: He's in frightening new territory—

Cat: "Our weary traveller—

Dog: "Without compass or map—

Cat:	"Stares about him—
Dog:	"Completely disorientated—
Cat:	"Black night, no stars to guide him—
Cat:	"Half choked with terror—
Dog:	"He wanders the homestead—

(They take a bow then turn to look at Hercules who is mooning about.)

Cat:	*(glumly)* We're saying he could live like this for years?
Dog:	You know he could. And NOT get his appetite back.
Cat:	You're teasing again! Please don't.
Dog:	Appetites are irregular, they come and go—
Cat:	Well, I'm fed up with burnt toast and mouldy jam. If he remembers the jam which you can't rely on.
Dog:	*(mimicking)* You're complaining again. Please don't.

Cat: *(twitching)* The worst is, he sets ME off. I'm getting fidgety. And you've heard my purring, I've lost all sense of rhythm. I DO NOT LIKE A DISORDERLY HOUSE.

Dog: Come on Cat, this is Britain, remember? Mustn't grumble.

Cat: I'll grumble if I feel like it. Which I do. I'm bored. Nothing's happening. We're standing still. Or going backwards! Losing our grip one step at a time. *(to Hercules)* Well, I'm not ready to give up. DO something! Run a marathon, rob a bank, sell your soul to the devil – something, anything –

Dog: *(shocked)* Cat!

Cat: I need action.

Dog: *(handing Cat a broom)* There you go.

(Dog starts tidying, arranging things on a shelf, folding up newspapers. Cat sweeps but then stops and leans on his broom.)

Cat: *(to Dog)* Hey, did you hear the one about the mother-in-law driving her—

(Hercules deliberately untidies things and takes Cat's broom away so Cat half falls.)

Hercules: What's the matter with you two? We're on a serious mission here. We don't have time for house cleaning.

Cat: Mission? What mission?

Dog: He means grieving for Hecuba.

Cat: *(sarcastically)* He means living in a mess and starving ourselves.

Hercules: It's proper mourning protocol. Look it up. Miserable rations, sleepless nights, wretched days, these are the minimum standard requirements.

Cat: Rubbish.

Hercules: We do everything by the book, we speak in low tones, we play sad music, we have a miserable funeral, in short we pay our debt to Hecuba in full and then we're FREE.

Cat: Are you kidding! You haven't been free since the day she turned your head forty odd years ago when you went down like a ninepin and if I remember correctly never got back up.

You mark my words, you'll never be free. The dead don't wander off into the mist never to be heard of again, they pop up everywhere, nonstop, often when you're least expecting them and not always in a good mood. You can't just snap your fingers and have them disappear at will, no sir, they're a persistent lot, they hang around. I bet the whole pack of your personal dead will be snapping at your heels until the day you die, with Hecuba leader of the gang.

Hercules: *(low voice)* I have to get free. I can't live like this.

Cat: Then put your accurate hat on! Accept how you feel. Glad, sorry, excited, scared—

Hercules: Glad?

Cat: OK, let's say up for a challenge.

Hercules: …no –

Cat: Come on, who doesn't like flirting with the idea of the new life that might be out there on the horizon … make your peace with the past, and in six months' time you could be selling the house, travelling, starting over.

Hercules: Starting over?

Cat: Why not?

Hecuba: *(Is standing with her hands on her hips, challenging Hercules.)*

Hercules: ...she wouldn't let me.

Cat: *(takes the globe off the table and spins it)* There. Choose your destination. Rome, Beijing, Timbuctoo—

(Hercules spins the globe, looking at places he might travel to.)

Hecuba: *(Takes it off him and puts it away.)*

Dog: Give her time.

Hercules: *(quietly, feeling old and confused)* I don't have time.

Dog: Things will change.

Hercules: But not Hecuba. Hecuba will always be looking over my shoulder. She'll never let go. Or forgive me.

Cat: *(crossly)* There's nothing to forgive.

Hercules: *(to Hecuba)* You won't, will you? Why should you? I wouldn't in your shoes.

Cat: You didn't DO anything.

Hercules: Why can't SOMETHING be perfect! A love affair, for example. Imagine it!

Dog: Perfect?

Hercules: *(angrily)* Not a word out of place! Nothing to be forgiven for, nothing to forgive. It has to be possible! Looking back over forty years all I see are big storms, little storms, friction, arguments that belittle us both, days of constant irritation—

Cat: Stop exaggerating.

Dog: I didn't hear you complaining at the time.

Hercules: *(bombastically)* Well, I'm complaining now. I want to look back and find not one speck of dirt or dust on our glorious past.

(Cat and Dog look at one another and sigh in unison.)

Dog: *(meaning it)* Poor Hercules!

Cat: *(not meaning it)* Poor Hercules.

Dog: Not one speck of dirt or dust in forty years!

Cat: I heard. The guy's crazy. *(to Hercules)* It's a dirty, dusty world, son. *(to Dog)* You know, I say we pack it in, down tools and leave the site. We're not doing any good here. The boss *(indicating Hercules)* is a dreamer, he wants the impossible, to construct a past without a single blemish on it. That's never going to happen. We're wasting our time.

Dog: But Cat—

(Hercules picks up a photo of Hecuba and is dreaming over it.)

Cat: Hold on. Here we go. Another huge mood swing.

Hercules: *(showing Cat the photo of Hecuba)* Our wedding day.

Cat: *(sighing)* On guard. Troops to attention. This is the lyrical phase coming up.

Hercules: *(showing the photo)* See how lovely she was.

Cat: *(to Dog wearily)* And there'll be more! Beautiful, perfect.

Hercules: She WAS beautiful.

Cat: *(sarcastically)* Sure, sang like a bird, danced like an angel—

Hercules: *(stubbornly)* Well, she did.

Cat: *(sarcastically)* Never once let you down, was the pride of ten counties, not one speck of dirt or dust on HER!

Hercules: *(getting a cat biscuit)* Puss, puss, puss—

(Cat comes hopping over for the food and Hercules gets him by the scruff of the neck and throws him into the wings. Hercules comes back dusting off his hands.)

Off with the heads of all traitors and rebels. *(turning to Hecuba)* Don't you worry, your majesty, we're loyal here, we'll see you right.

(Cat comes limping back.)

Dog: *(to Cat)* Let him dream. What else does he have!

Cat: He's crippled me. *(to Hercules)* Stop WORSHIPPING her. It's not normal.

Hercules: *(to Hecuba, to annoy Cat)* Oh mighty queen, you will reign for ever in my heart.

Cat: *(to Hecuba)* Beware. Old man speak with forked tongue. Right now he'd say anything to get on your good side. Doesn't mean five minutes down the line he won't be calling you a bitch again. In death as in life.

Hecuba: *(Is troubled by what Cat is saying and moves away from Hercules.)*

Cat: That's my girl. You be careful.

Hecuba: *(Retreats further.)*

Hercules: *(angrily to Hecuba)* Stay where you are. There! There! You don't come and go without my permission. *(a bit mad)* It confuses me.

Cat: *(sarcastically to Dog)* Whadda y'know! Our boy's confused.

Dog: Poor fellow, too tired to think straight.

Cat: Think! Hercules? I wish!

Hecuba: (*Moves away.*)

Hercules: (*very lethargically, mumbling and rambling*) OK, go. Don't go ... what do I care ... I don't care ...

Dog: We're losing him again. Oops, he's going under.

(*Hercules half faints, Dog fans Hercules and loosens his shirt, Hercules stares straight ahead. Cat snaps his fingers at Hercules, who does not respond. Dog picks up Hercules' arm and lets it flop.*)

I think he's dying.

Cat: Well, he's not.

(*Hercules groans.*)

Dog: Wants to say a few last words.

Cat: He is NOT dying. Why do you always have to imagine the worst?

Dog: It would look very romantic on his cv. "Here lies Hercules, died three days after Hecuba, of a broken heart."

Cat: *(to Hercules)* Get up. You have unfinished business to attend to. Come ON!

(Hercules flops more. Dog paces, thinking.)

Dog: … OK, here's a variation on the plumbing idea. He often worries about money, right?

Cat: Right.

Dog: How about a stiff letter from the bank manager telling him if he doesn't pay his bills he'll have the bailiffs at the door?

Cat: *(acting Hercules)* "Oh my god, the bailiffs are at the door, ruin stares me in the face."

Dog: "The house will be repossessed, I'll be evicted and out on the street."

Cat: *(acting Hercules)* "I'll die in the workhouse."

Dog: He wakes up, showers, brushes his teeth, smooths his hair and is off to the bank to settle the matter.

Cat: Gets him out of the house.

Dog: Gives him something new to think about. He sees people going about their business, figures the world is on course as usual and that maybe there's a place in it for him. It might waken a spark of energy.

Cat: … and it might not. It might be the last straw. Instead of rushing into action to save his financial situation, he declines the challenge, he tears up the letter, pretends it never existed and lets himself sink still deeper—

Cat: Into the murky waters of the dark lagoon.

Dog: Into the murky waters of the dark lagoon.

Cat: Let's go for it. *(taking a letter from the desk and handing it to Hercules)* You haven't paid the bills.

(Hercules shrugs.)

Dog: We'll have the bailiffs at the door.

(Hercules shrugs.)

You'll be turned out of the house. *(whispering)* The neighbours will know. Your reputation will be in tatters.

(Hercules shrugs.)

You'll be homeless.

Cat: Walking the streets and sleeping rough.

Dog: Kicked, spat on, despised.

Hercules: *(very lethargically)* Don't care.

(a pause)

Cat: *(exasperated)* It's your line!

(Hercules shrugs.)

"I'll die in the workhouse."

Hercules: *(mumbling lethargically, can hardly be heard)* Die in the work house.

Cat: *(to the audience)* OK, now for our next trick.

(Cat and Dog walk away arm in arm, then suddenly turn round.)

Cat: *(in unison, very loudly)* Boo.

Dog: *(in unison, very loudly)* Boo.

(Hercules jumps out of his skin, is very alive and very angry. He shakes his fist at them.)

>   That looks like a normal reaction to me.

Cat: Well, well, the old Hercules is still in there somewhere.

Dog: So there's hope?

Cat: Hope? Dirty word. Wash your mouth out.

(Cat and Dog march Hercules up and down to keep him focussed.)

Hercules: *(wearily)* I should never have married.

Cat: Yeah, well, you did.

(a slight pause, Hercules is abstracted)

Hercules: I couldn't let somebody else get their hands on her.

Dog: Of course not.

Hercules: *(working himself into a rage)* I'd have killed him.

Cat: The dirty dog.

Hercules: Or her!

Cat: *(sarcastically)* Rotten whore!

Hercules: Or both! *(working himself up)* Shot them clean through the head! Or heart! Or taken a knife to them—

Dog: *(seriously)* The bastards!

Hercules: Bastards! Stupid pricks! *(working himself up wildly, pointing at the audience)* How dare you look at my wife that way! I know what you're up to—

(Cat makes an he's crazy gesture.)

Cat: *(to Dog)* Lock the door.

Dog: Eh?

Cat: No one in, no one out until he's calmed down and come to his senses.

(Dog locks the door and hands the key to Cat.)

Hercules: *(to Hecuba)* You did it on purpose. You put on a new dress, you did up your hair, you simpered and smirked, of course they came buzzing around.

Cat: *(to Dog quietly)* This is pure fantasy.

Dog: Not all of it. He WAS jealous.

Cat: Hercules, your wife is innocent of any simpering! Stop making a fool of yourself.

Hercules: Innocent! Hecuba!

Cat: Yes.

Hercules: She humiliated me.

Cat: You humiliated yourself.

Hercules: *(glumly to Hecuba)* You LIKED making me make a fool of myself.

Hecuba: *(Shakes her head sadly.)*

Hercules: Yes, you did! And I was fool enough to let you.

Hecuba: *(Shakes her head wearily.)*

Hercules: I was just a kid. What did I know of the world! Nothing. If anyone was innocent ... *(breaks off)* But you knew everything. You took advantage of me.

Cat: Wait a minute. Wait a minute. Let's stick to reality here.

Dog: She was young, she liked to look pretty, to show off a little. It didn't mean anything.

Hercules: *(to himself)* It meant everything. I put my trust in a false God.

(Cat rolls his eyes. Dog feels Hercules forehead and finds it sweaty.)

Dog: Come on, you're feverish. You need to keep warm. *(putting a blanket around Hercules)* All that was a long time ago.

Hercules: I know. In the early days. But I remember it like it was yesterday.

Dog: Well, don't remember it.

Hercules: I can't stop myself.

Dog: *(seriously)* It only upsets you.

Hecuba: *(Raises her hand, demanding attention.)*

Dog: I know, you've been wrongly accused?

Hecuba: *(Nods.)*

Dog: You never looked at another man?

Hecuba: *(Shakes her head.)*

Cat: You seek redress?

Hecuba: *(Nods.)*

Dog: *(putting a wig on Cat's head)* The court is now in session.

Cat: For the claimant?

Dog: *(reading a document)* Hecuba, now deceased, but formerly of this parish, has been falsely accused by her husband of publicly humiliating him by her flirtatious behaviour, with the malicious intent of making him jealous.

Cat: *(to Hecuba)* And you deny the accusation?

Hecuba: *(Nods flirtatiously.)*

Cat: *(to Hecuba)* Behave yourself. (to Dog) When did these events occur?

Dog: They go back more than forty years, your honour.

Cat: I need details.

Dog: Sorry my Lord, it's too long ago to recall. Hercules has a hazy sense of injustice is about all he can offer by way of detail.

Cat: *(pointing to Hercules)* We all have a hazy sense of injustice. I find for the claimant.

Hercules: You haven't heard the evidence.

Cat: I never hear the evidence. It confuses me. And it will make no difference to the sentence. A higher court than mine has already made its decision. Attention!

(Hercules stands to attention.)

Loneliness.

Hercules: Huh?

Hecuba: *(Claps.)*

Cat: Loneliness is the sentence. The court will rise and the prisoner be returned to his cell.

(Hercules groans.)

Where considering your age you'll probably die. Best to be prepared. Take a walking stick, hearing aid, incontinence pads with you. And a word of caution. Hide your valuables now from thieving lawyers and carers – and no dreaming of parole. This is for life.

Hercules: Mercy, my Lord?

Cat: Mercy? Out of the question.

Hercules: I'm an old man, my Lord.

Cat: Which leaves you very little time to repent.

Hercules: I HAVE repented.

Cat: That's what you say, but where's the proof?

Hercules: The tears I've shed, my lord?

Cat: Tears? I've got no faith in tears. Anyway the sentence can't be changed, you will die in custody.

Hercules: *(low voice)* No hope of an appeal??

Cat: Certainly not. Waste of the court's time. Your doom has been pronounced! *(taking off his wig and going back to his usual self)* And there you have it.

Dog: According to my calculations that makes it six nil to Hecuba.

(Cat and Hercules nod glumly.)

… *(hesitantly)* … there ARE alternative scenarios … or so I've heard …

Hercules: *(glumly)* Oh, like what?

Dog: Well, "Hecuba and I had a wonderful relationship" would be one example.

(gesturing Hercules to join in)

Hercules: *(disbelievingly)* Hecuba and I had a wonderful relationship?

Dog: Why not? "We met, married, and lived happily ever after."

Hercules: Lived happily ever after?

Dog: Exactly. Her death was painless.

Hercules: Her death was painless

Dog: It was all over quickly, she had no time to panic.

Hercules: *(joining in)* No time to panic.

Dog: She never suffered and I – that's you – can rest easy.

Hercules: *(joining in)* She never suffered and I – that's me – can rest easy.

(Dog nods encouragingly.)

"Nothing to look back on but beautiful memories."

Dog: See, it's simple once you know how.

Cat: Did I hear her death was painless?

Dog: It could have been.

Cat: Who are we trying to kid here?

Dog: She might have found peace, and agreed to go quietly.

Cat: Hecuba?

Hercules: Why not? "A wonderful relationship." Sounds good. I like it.

Cat: Sounds good! Is that all that matters to you? Have neither of you ANY interest in accuracy?

Dog: *(seriously)* Not really.

Cat: Shame on you.

Dog: You don't KNOW she suffered.

Cat: You don't KNOW she didn't.

(Hercules looks helplessly from one to the other.)

Did.

Dog: Didn't.

Cat: Did.

Dog: Didn't.

(Hercules bewildered, wails. They both turn on him.)

Dog: Shut up.

Cat: Shut up.

Hercules: *(quietly to himself)* I'm going mad.

Cat: *(fed up with the conversation)* Meow. Meow. Meow. Meow. Meow.

Dog: Woof. Woof. Woof. Woof.

(It's mayhem.)

Hercules: *(bowing down to Hecuba)* I'm begging you! Put me out of my misery. Tell me it was easy.

Cat: You are not kneeling to Hecuba. HER DAY IS DONE.

Hercules: *(to Hecuba)* Help me!

Cat: THE QUEEN IS DEAD. There's a new regime to answer to. *(like a seer)* "Beware sire, the moon has a bloody aspect, your advisers are not to be trusted. Fly the realm, say good bye to the dead lying on this field of battle, bury the past, find a new country and start again, a refugee in a strange world with different habits and different expectations. Don't expect to be happy, if you leave everything you love behind, how are you going to be happy? You're a migrant for one reason only, the old country has gone up in flames and there's nothing there for you. And remember, sire, not all migrants settle, they can't, the longing for their own country is always with them, they can never sever the old allegiances …" *(breaks off, then briskly, in a different tone)* In short, It's going to be tough.

Hecuba: *(Makes a flirtatious, attention seeking gesture.)*

Cat: *(watching Hecuba)* Here we go. The siren call of the old regime.

(Hercules responds to Hecuba. Cat wags a finger at her.)

Madam, your reign is over.

Hecuba: *(Draws herself up and makes a power salute.)*

Cat: You heard. He'll be off on his travels.

Hecuba: *(Gives Cat the finger.)*

Cat: And if you don't behave he won't take his memories of you with him.

Hecuba: *(Wags her finger at Cat.)*

Cat: "My wife? Oh her. Hardly remember what she looks like. Don't want HER around spoiling the party."

Hecuba: *(Shakes her head vigorously.)*

Cat: You'd be surprised how quickly they can forget.

Hecuba: *(Sticks her tongue out at Cat.)*

Cat: He'd soon see he could do without you. So you stay on your best behaviour, my lady, or you'll be shown the door. He's not going to put up with your tantrums for ever. He'll be saying to himself, "Done my duty by her, I can't do more," and he'll turn his back. He won't have time for you. He'll be out on the town with his friends.

Hecuba: *(Shakes her head vigorously.)*

Cat: OK, making eyes at the rich widow.

Hecuba: *(Gives Cat the finger and then goes to make eyes at Hercules.)*

Cat: *(to Hecuba)* Don't be so needy.

Dog: *(to Cat)* Yeah, well, don't you be so rough.

Hecuba: *(Beckons to Hercules.)*

(Hercules moves mechanically towards her and follows her as she moves away, as though he's on a lead.)

Dog: This won't do. *(to Hercules)* Come away, old fellow.

(Hercules looks from Hecuba to Dog, he doesn't know which to follow, he's confused, he chooses Hecuba.)

She's not letting go.

Cat: More fool Hecuba!

Dog: *(to Cat sadly)* Nothing to be done, I suppose. He HAS to suffer.

Cat: Which means another twenty four hours without a meal! *(nostalgically)* Back in the day, they didn't come sleeker than me. I was famous all over the neighbourhood for sleekness, but that's regular meals and a good night's sleep … … I'm deteriorating, Dog.

Dog: Me too. My coat's losing its shine, my eye is dull—

(Dog and Cat sit glumly.)

Hecuba: *(Is making a praying, beseeching gesture to Hercules.)*

Cat: *(watching Hecuba)* It's just want, want, want with some people.

Hecuba: *(Points to her watch.)*

Dog: Needs another twenty four hours back with him to set the record straight.

Cat: *(to Hecuba)* Is that right, pet?

Hecuba: *(Nods.)*

Dog: Enough time to say sorry.

Cat: Yeah well, that's not how it goes.

Hecuba: *(Stands arms akimbo being aggressive.)*

Cat: *(mimicking her aggression)* And none of that. You're a ghost, you're here on sufferance. You don't HAVE rights.

Hecuba: *(Sulks.)*

Cat: He has business to attend to.

Hecuba: *(Shrugs.)*

Cat: Look at him, the stupid fellow is already half out of his mind with grief, why add to his troubles with your troubles. Show mercy.

Hecuba: *(Beckons in a majestic manner to Hercules.)*

(Hercules follows her and she leads him around like a dog on a lead.)

Cat: *(sarcastically)* "Non, je suis La Grande Dame Sans Merci!" Good Boy. Now sit, beg, roll over.

(Hercules puts his paws together and pants like a dog, looking up at Hecuba.)

Hecuba: *(Tosses back her head flirtatiously.)*

Cat: *(to Hercules)* Thinks she's twenty again, silly girl. Don't you fall for it.

Hercules: *(offering Hecuba his hand)* Come.

(Hecuba puts out a hand but they don't connect.)

"Let us arise and go now, and go to Innisfree, And a small cabin build there—"

(Hecuba and Hercules move to exit, Hecuba triumphant.)

Cat: *(interrupting, talking to Hercules)* OK, fine, off you go, but you're not leaving before you've registered the death, probated the will, settled her insurance policy, packed up the house—

(Dog detaches Hecuba from Hercules and marches her away.)

Hecuba: *(Sulks.)*

Cat: Organised the funeral, dug the grave, ordered the flowers, bought yourself a new suit to wear for the occasion, sworn a solemn oath never to write another poem—

Dog: *(very seriously)* Or design another mausoleum.

Hercules: *(ears pricking up)* What was that?

Cat: Hmm?

Hercules: *(interested)* … a new suit?

Cat: Well?

Hercules: I thought I heard a new suit.

Dog: You did.

Hercules: Got a fancy for a new suit.

Hecuba: *(Rolls her eyes.)*

Dog: *(aside to Cat)* Well done. Brilliant. That's the first sign of life he's shown for days. Maybe this is the break through. Maybe we're finally getting somewhere. *(talking to Hercules as to a child)* Think of it. A whole new outfit you can choose yourself!

Cat: How about a deal? Today you start sorting through her stuff, not all of it's junk, tomorrow we hit town to buy you a suit, a good suit, no expense spared—.

Hercules: *(like Lady Bracknell)* JUNK! Did I hear JUNK!

Cat: I said, not all! Some of it could be sold.

Hercules: Sold!

Cat: Or go to a charity shop.

Hercules: EVERYTHING STAYS!

Dog: *(to Hercules)* I don't understand. You've been wanting to declutter for years, now's your chance.

Hercules: Are you mad? NOTHING THAT HECUBA EVER TOUCHED IS LEAVING THIS HOUSE.

Cat: *(holding up an old newspaper)* Nothing?

Hercules: *(taking the newspaper away from Cat and cradling it)* Nothing!

Cat: *(in unison, very glumly)* Ah.

Dog: *(in unison, very glumly)* Ah.

Cat: Not the breakthrough we were looking for.

Dog: *(trying to be cheerful)* ... he wants a new suit, remember! That's positive.

Cat: Well, he's not getting one if he won't do a deal.

Dog: *(to Hercules)* Come on, you like the place tidy—

Hercules: Don't nag.

Cat: It has to be a trade off. You get a new suit, with all the trimmings, tie, shirt, etcetera, but the junk has to go.

Dog: *(to Hercules)* Her knick knacks do collect a lot of dust ... *(no reply)* they're a health hazard, you'd be better off without them.

Hercules: *(grandly)* I don't care about dust.

Dog: You do when it sets your allergies off. You sneeze fit to bust. You'll give yourself a hernia one of these days.

Hercules: You can NOT get a hernia from sneezing.

Dog: *(seriously)* No and you can NOT save yourself by keeping the place exactly as she left it.

(a short pause)

Hercules: *(grandly)* It won't be exactly as she left it. No sir, there are going to be changes.

Cat: Sounds ominous. Cross your fingers.

Hercules: *(grandly)* I'm going to turn it into a museum.

Cat: *(sotto voce)* Not in my lifetime.

Hercules: *(not listening)* And not to save me, to save HER! It's my responsibility to provide a memorial for her. Nobody else is going to. When I die who will remember her? She's to be remembered ... they're all to be remembered *(confused)* ... all of them ... they're not to vanish ... they must all be accounted for ... *(getting more and more anxious)*

(Cat and Dog exchange glances and gesture he's acting crazy.)

Dog: ... what colour are you thinking?

Hercules: Huh?

Dog: For the suit?

Hercules: What suit?

Dog: The one you're buying for the funeral.

Hercules: I don't know what you're talking about.

Dog: The suit for her funeral.

Hercules: *(not listening)* The pictures she liked will be here, *(indicating the wall)* the photos of her here, items of value in the cabinet, all properly labelled. Her life will be traced from its beginning –

Cat: *(tartly)* Hercules, whatever you do now when its time comes this house will be bull dozed, bombed, fall into ruins, sink beneath a tidal wave, be disassembled, taken apart until there is nothing left of either it or her. She WILL disappear, vanish, be forgotten! *(turning to Hecuba)* Nothing personal, sweetheart.

Hercules: I won't let her disappear. I'll carve her name on every tree, draw it on every city wall, I'll fight for her til my last breath. She stays.

Cat: The trees will die, the city walls be razed, no one stays.

Dog: Be generous. Let him dream.

Cat: Anyway, you'll probably marry again in a couple of years and forget all about her. *(to Hecuba)* That would put the cat among the pigeons, eh, ma belle?

Hercules: Don't be impertinent.

Cat: Nothing wrong with marrying again.

Dog: *(seriously)* It's never too late to be setting out on a new adventure.

Hercules: I don't want a new adventure. I want HER.

Hecuba: *(Preens.)*

Cat: Well, don't kid yourself you're going to like living on your own with a ghost, because you won't.

Dog: Cat's right, you'll be miserable.

Cat: Of course I'm right—

Hercules: *(very angrily)* Leave me alone, all of you. My future is none of your business.

(Hecuba, Dog and Cat wag their fingers at Hercules.)

(shouting) From now on I do what I want. *(change of mood, pitifully)* I don't KNOW what I want. We do things TOGETHER. *(to Hecuba)* Don't go.

Hecuba: *(Is distressed, mimes tears.)*

Cat: Tears won't help. He has a new life now.

Hecuba: *(Nods her head sadly.)*

Dog: *(seriously, to Hecuba)* Ah! You're scared he's going to make a mess of it?

Hecuba: *(Nods.)*

Dog: You worry about him?

Hecuba: *(Nods.)*

Dog: How he'll cope? For example, the suit he's going to buy for himself? Chances are it'll be a disaster.

Hecuba: *(Nods.)*

Dog: And the same for more important decisions?

Hecuba: *(Groans.)*

Dog: It's true. There are choppy waters ahead. No way round it. *(tidying Hecuba's dress and smoothing her hair)* My advice? Smarten up, look your best, turn on the charm. You want to hang around, Cat's right again, no tears. It's not a long face Hercules is looking for, it's Hecuba the Brave!

Hecuba: *(Tidies her hair, then does a twirl.)*

Dog: That's my girl.

Hecuba: *(Twirls in front of Hercules who does not pay attention because he is anxiously trying to write.)*

Dog: *(to Hercules)* No, no no.

Cat: *(looking over Hercules' shoulder)* A new and even sillier poem.

(Hercules shows it to Cat, Dog and Hecuba who give it the thumbs down.)

Dog: No.

Cat: *(taking the page of paper off Hercules)* Give it up. There's no way to explain to people how much she meant to you. It's a lost cause.

Hercules: … I can't give it up. Not before I've made a statement of everything I owe her.

Hecuba: *(Claps.)*

Cat: *(very sceptically)* And how are you going to do that?

Hercules: *(glumly)* No idea, but she thinks I have it in me.

Cat: *(to Hecuba, very sceptically)* You do?

Hecuba: *(Nods.)*

Hercules: *(very glumly)* She thinks I can manage without her.

Cat: *(to Hecuba)* You're joking?

Hecuba: *(Shakes her head.)*

Hercules: *(glumly)* She's always had illusions about me. About what I'm capable of.

Cat:	Oh, come on, the woman's not a fool.
Hercules:	*(very glumly)* She BELIEVES in me.
Cat:	*(incredulously)* After forty years?
Hecuba:	*(Nods.)*
Cat:	*(to Hecuba)* Are you crazy?
Hecuba:	*(Shakes her head.)*
Cat:	After all that's come and gone?
Hecuba:	*(Smiles and nods.)*
Cat:	*(aside to Dog)* It must be love. *(to Hecuba)* So what do you fancy for your future?
Hecuba:	*(Considers.)*
Dog:	*(very seriously)* How about no more regrets, griefs, bitching, from either of you?
Hecuba:	*(Nods.)*
Cat:	You let him sleep. And snore. And eat his dinner in peace. You give him some space. And you stop HAUNTING him.
Hecuba:	*(Nods.)*

(Hercules nods.)

Cat: *(to Hercules)* As for you! It's easy! You live by the best of her!

Hercules: Yes sir.

Cat: No mausoleums, no poetry, no six black horses to draw her coffin.

(Hercules nods.)

You clean up the house. You take Dog for a walk and you get back to work and you make a life for yourself.

Hercules: Yes sir.

Cat: *(to Hercules and Hecuba)* So what do you say? Do we have a deal?

(Hecuba, Hercules and Dog nod.)

We're agreed?

Hercules: Yes sir.

Dog: Yes sir.

Hecuba: *(Nods.)*

Cat: All in favour?

(They all put up their hands.)

Then let the last dance begin.

(Hecuba and Hercules smile at one another and dance. It's a good moment. Cat and Dog watch satisfied.)

MOUSE THE UNREADY

Mouse: in his seventies and suffering from a serious heart problem
Omega: Death
Malik: Mouse's alter ego

The scene is Mouse's shabby living room. Omega is dressed in black like Death and carries a scythe.

(*Mouse squeaks.*)

Omega: What's YOUR problem?

Mouse: I'm a very little creature, I live in a corner someplace, nothing fancy—

Omega: Well?

Mouse: I've been thinking, since I'm no trouble to anyone, that I might be excused dying.

Omega: Excused dying?

Mouse: If you please.

Omega: No.

Mouse: It's the children, sir.

Omega: What children?

Mouse: My children. They need me here to keep an eye on them. You know how it is with kids.

Omega: No.

Mouse: And after them there's the grandchildren to be thought of—

Omega: *(sarcastically)* And then the great grandchildren, I suppose, and the great great grandchildren.

Mouse: I'm a speck on the landscape, I don't see it would do you any harm to give me say another—

Omega: *(sarcastically)* Fifty years?

Mouse: I was going to suggest a hundred. That would really take the pressure off. I could relax and go back to enjoying myself the way I used to.

Omega: No.

Mouse: *(insouciantly)* Come on, there's not that much wrong with me.

Omega: Yes, there is. I checked the doctor's report.

Mouse: The odd dizzy moment now and again, that's all.

Omega Don't pretend you didn't hear what she said.

Mouse: She mumbled.

Omega: She was warning you.

Mouse: *(trying to usher Omega out of the room, and speaking with an Irish voice)* Top o' the morning to yer!

Omega: I'm staying.

Mouse: What do you mean?

Omega: I'm taking up residence here.

Mouse: You can't do that.

Omega: Why not?

(Omega hones his scythe.)

Mouse: Because watching you sharpen that thing is dulling my sense of security, and causing a lot of unnecessary stress.

Omega: I like sharpening it.

Mouse: If you could look at it from my point of view you'd see I'm getting a miniscule scrap of the universe's timespan. I've hardly had time to turn around and there you are ... sharpening!

(Omega continues to sharpen assiduously.)

	The fact is that at the moment I'm just not up for it.
Omega:	Up for what?
Mouse:	Dying, idiot! I need to be in a better mood. I think we should reschedule.
Omega:	I never reschedule.
Mouse:	*(put out)* Oh! Cancel?
Omega:	I never cancel and I never negotiate.
Mouse:	But think of the suffering you cause.
Omega:	Suffering is not my problem. I'm a simple servant to the laws of nature, nothing more and nothing less.
Mouse:	*(crossly)* Bother nature! … look, old fellow, I have commitments. For example, I've promised myself to vote in the election next month.
Omega:	Vote? In your situation, why bother?
Mouse:	It's my civic duty. I worry the country might go to the dogs without my input. The same goes for the family.

Omega: Oh hubris, thy name is Mouse.

Mouse: *(not understanding)* Eh?

(Mouse suddenly feels ill and groans.)

Omega: *(hopefully)* Heart bothering you?

Mouse: *(grumpily)* No.

Omega: You sure? It didn't look good on the X-ray.

Mouse: It's fine.

Omega: That's not what the doc said.

Mouse: Ohhhhhhhhhh.

Omega: Will is in order?

(Mouse is suffering.)

Might be the moment to call the family.

Mouse: No.

(Mouse groans loudly.)

Omega: *(wielding his scythe ready)* I can make my move any time—

Mouse: *(shouting)* No!

Omega: *(wagging a finger at him)* Hey, mind your manners, old man.

Mouse: I'm in pain.

Omega: And bow your head before you speak to me.

Mouse: I am NOT bowing!

Omega: A dignified bow is OK.

Mouse: No it isn't.

Omega: Come on, make it easy on yourself, accept the inevitable.

Mouse: *(looking around)* But I'm used to it here – the planet I mean – TV, reading, the pleasures of the table, consciousness, the whole caboodle, it's familiar territory, not perfect, what is? … how about a compromise, say another ten years—

Omega: Ah, but it might be a different ten years. Ten years of pain and disability. You've been reasonably lucky so far, why risk it? *(quietly)* People can long for me, remember!

Mouse: If you're trying to frighten me, that's not fair.

Omega: *(singing from the Mikado)* "I'm the lord high executioner!"

Mouse: Here I am in my prime—

Omega: Spectacles, hearing aid, can't walk without a stick?

Mouse: My emotional prime! I'm patient, understanding, hardly ever lose my temper. Now to get back to our negotiations—

Omega: What negotiations?

Mouse: My extra fifty years.

Omega: Nothing doing.

Mouse: For the children's sake.

Omega: No.

Mouse: … how about if my country needs me?

Omega: It doesn't need you.

Mouse: You don't know that.

Omega: Yes, I do. You're old.

(Mouse tries to stand up straight, he has to hold onto his cane.)

Come on, you don't fool ME.

Mouse: OK, I'm rickety on the outside but on the inside I'm like a new blush rose, sweet-scented, full of promise—

Omega: *(nauseated)* Oh, please!

Mouse: *(waving his cane and the hearing aid etc)* Don't look at this. This isn't me.

Omega: Mouse—

Mouse: *(trembling)* It's a pastiche of me.

Omega: Mouse—

Mouse: A cruel caricature.

Omega: Mouse—

Mouse: When I think what I was.

Omega: Mouse, you're costing society.

Mouse: No.

Omega: That fall you had last month, that didn't come cheap.

Mouse: That was an accident. Could have happened to anyone.

Omega: You tripped.

Mouse: Lots of people trip.

Omega: Lots of people over seventy.

Mouse: Look—

Omega: Face it, your day is over, my friend

Mouse: Let's do a deal. Let's shake on, say, five years. And I'm not your friend.

Omega: Not five, not four—

Mouse: Months?

(Omega shakes his head.)

Weeks?

(Omega wags a finger at him.)

I've got a wish list this long—

Omega: Of course you do.

(Omega is half looking out of the window. Mouse steals the scythe and tries to hide it.)

(without looking round) Put it back.

(Mouse tests the scythe's edge.)

Mouse: On the dull side.

Omega: Sharp enough for you, Mousie.

Mouse: Maybe you'd like to hear about my next project before setting a date for my departure.

Omega: Well, I wouldn't.

(a slight pause)

Mouse: *(grandly)* OK, here's an idea. How about you throw caution to the winds and decide to let me live FOREVER!

Omega: Not on my watch.

Mouse: I AM NOT READY TO GO.

Malik: My suggestion? Balance your accounts, make your confession, and say your goodbyes.

(Mouse gives Malik the finger.)

... so how do they look?

Mouse: How does what look?

Malik: Your accounts. You have a decent balance?

Mouse: *(sulkily)* I don't know

Malik: You're not in debt I hope?

Mouse: *(haughtily)* I don't DO accounts.

Malik : Well, now's the time.

(Mouse turns his back.)

Come on, let's see your last month's statement. Well, don't just stand there. Go and get it! ... ... I know you know where it is.

(Mouse drags his feet going to fetch the statement.)

Hurry up. We don't have all day.

Mouse: *(panicking)* We don't?

Malik: *(teasing)* Well, probably we do, but who knows!

(Mouse hands the statement to Malik sulkily.)

Don't be embarrassed. *(studying it)* Be embarrassed. This is a mess. Look, if you're planning to die easy you're going to have to get busy. Shift the balance of payments a little. Less on the debit side, more on the credit side.

Mouse: Oh, and how am I supposed to do that?

Malik: Well, there are a number of ways. You could stop squabbling with the neighbours—

Mouse: No, I couldn't.

Malik: Be straight with the tax man—

Mouse: Even less.

Malik: Get on better terms with your son in law?

Mouse: Never.

(Omega leans towards Mouse and puts his hands on his shoulders and stares at him.)

Take your filthy hands off me.

Omega: *(like a sorcerer, sarcastically)* I am The Master. Look deep into my eyes and reform while there is still time.

(Mouse is pulling away and trying to avoid looking at Omega.)

(like a sorcerer) Stop wriggling.

Mouse: *(stopping wriggling)* OK. OK ... Omega?

Omega: Well?

Mouse: I have a query.

Omega: *(bowing)* Well?

Mouse: Could you explain to me, please, what it's like to be dead?

Omega: You wouldn't understand, you're a mouse.

Mouse: Eh?

Omega: A tiny, insignificant being, incapable of understanding anything, the universe, infinity, dying—

Mouse: Me! Insignificant!

Omega: On a global scale almost invisible.

Mouse: *(not listening)* The fact is I worry I may have wasted my life.

Omega: There's always waste.

Mouse: And if I do have to die – I don't see the necessity myself – I'm not clear on the procedure.

Omega: *(airily)* Nothing to it. I do all the work. You just lie back and enjoy the ride.

Mouse: *(very sarcastically)* Thank you.

Omega: But I do have a couple of suggestions.

Mouse: Eh?

Omega: Keep the house tidy, and wear something decent—

Mouse: Eh?

Omega: *(ghostly, hollow voice)* In case I strike without warning. When you're alone. I've done the deed, a neighbor enters, relative, concerned citizen, there you are, a corpse on the floor, shock, ooo, *(screaming dramatically)* neighbor looks closer, finds it's a well-cared for corpse, nicely dressed, in the pink so to speak as corpses go, it might—

Mouse: *(very sarcastically)* Soften the blow?

Omega: Neighbor will say to him or herself "No need for any extravagant grief here, this one was ready."

Mouse: Yeah, well, I want the neighbour to know that I wasn't ready, that I was very unready. Mouse the Unready.

Omega: *(interrupting)* OK, how about a compromise. Clean underwear.

Mouse: Eh?

Omega: Your underwear is a disgrace. Never seen such a tangle of threadbare rubbish. You should throw the whole lot away and get something cheerful—

Mouse: *(very sarcastically)* To die in?

Omega: Would make a good last impression.

(Mouse looks at himself in the mirror.)

Mouse: ... you know the cat winks at me these days? My dried up old carcass is not worth the hunting.

Omega: My puir wee mousey.

Mouse: *(sighing heavily)* Well, that's what they say, right, pride goes before a fall and heaven knows in our prime we're proud enough. Strutting about the universe like we own it.

Omega: *(rubbing his hands together)* But the years pass and then people who've never paid the slightest attention to me suddenly find themselves in a cold sweat. I have to laugh.

Mouse: *(bravely)* I need more time.

Omega: More time? At seventy plus, with your medical records? Not likely.

Mouse: *(fussing)* I have a million things to do.

Omega: Of course you do.

Mouse: Everything's in disorder, my papers, personal effects, my estate—

Omega: Mouse, you've had years to get yourself sorted—

Mouse: But I'm not sorted.

Omega: … try thinking of it as a noble sacrifice.

Mouse: Eh?

Omega: Hopelessly overcrowded planet, inadequate infrastructure, old mice an awful strain on the system. Accept it's time to go.

Mouse: No.

Omega: Would look good on your cv.

Mouse: *(pettishly)* I don't care about my cv.

Omega: You're here on sufferance.

Mouse: *(indignantly)* Not at all. I'm independent. I pay my way.

Omega: *(putting on his glasses and looking at his notebook)* It says here, "Expendable. Mouse contributes nothing to the nation's GDP and given Alzheimers or some other mind altering ailment risks being a serious financial liability."

Mouse: *(angry)* There is nothing wrong with my mind.

Omega: Yes there is, if you think you're useful to anyone.

Mouse: I'll compromise. Let's say another twenty—

Omega: *(interrupting)* Weeks?

Mouse: Years!

Omega: Another twenty years and you'd be riding around in a wheelchair, wearing diapers.

Mouse: Fine by me!

Omega: Gibbering, incontinent—

Mouse: *(cheerfully)* Plus I'd have no responsibilities, all my needs would be taken care of—

Omega: You wouldn't like it.

Mouse: But I'll love dying!

Malik: It would make a change.

Mouse: Shut up, Malik!

(Mouse pretends to sleep and snores a little.)

Omega: *(shouting in Mouse's ear)* Stop snoring.

Mouse: No.

Omega: Yeah, well, you're not sitting there half asleep pretending to ignore me.

Mouse: You know, I think you're making a mistake, old fellow. This is the wrong house.

Omega: No mistake.

Mouse: It's Mrs Snodgrass next door you want.

Omega: *(pointing with a bony finger)* Yooooo!

Mouse: No, no, no. Mrs S is ninety five if she's a day. She has dementia. It would be a kindness to take her. Her family would be grateful. She's in a miserable state. She'd be glad to go.

Omega: *(singing)* "I want you, you, you."

Mouse: I'm eighteen years younger.

Omega: I've made my decision.

Mouse: You're mad. That woman can hardly move, *(pathetically proud)* I can still get up the stairs all on my own.

Omega: Not for much longer.

Mouse: My faculties are functioning perfectly—

Omega: *(sceptically)* Perfectly? You're half blind, partly deaf—

Mouse: *(grumbling)* I can still do the crossword, manage my bills. I'm not the priority here. Have I ever been any bother? No. What difference would another couple of years make to the world?

Omega: I've made my decision.

Mouse: Come on, Mrs S, put your hand up, say it, "It's my turn."

Malik: Leave the woman alone.

Mouse: Who'd miss her!

Malik: *(under his breath)* Who'd miss you!

Omega: On this street you're next, and that's it.

Mouse: *(muttering)* Crazy.

(Omega sharpens his scythe and whistles while he does it. Mouse is moving backwards and forwards in time to Omega's movements.)

>   … does it hurt?

Omega: Does what hurt?

Mouse: The operation …

Omega: What operation?

Mouse: The big one … the one that detaches me from existence?

Omega: Oh, that!

Mouse: Is it quick? What instruments of torture do you use? I'd like the facts.

(Omega shrugs.)

You must know.

Omega: Try the internet

(Mouse gives Omega the finger.)

Or the encyclopedia Britannica if you prefer print.

Mouse: *(crossly)* I've looked. There's nothing.

Omega: *(airily)* Well, don't you worry about it. You just put yourself into my hands—

Mouse: *(sarcastically)* Thank you!

Omega: And I take care of everything, the where, when, how—

(Mouse hands Omega a document.)

Mouse: First application for a delay.

Omega: *(tearing it up)* There are no delays in my court.

(Mouse points his fingers at Omega, like a gun. Omega puts up his hands, he's teasing.)

Mouse: *(ranting)* This is a busy year, my daughter will be forty, there are celebrations planned, a big family get together, cousins from abroad, children I've never seen before, I am not missing it.

Omega: Please, this isn't a public meeting.

Mouse: *(still ranting)* My family needs me. I am not turning my back on them.

Omega: Bravo.

Mouse: *(holding out his hand)* Look, I'm an honourable citizen. Couldn't we come up with a deal we can both agree on – say three years – and then I promise I won't back out when the time's up.

Omega: *(not taking Mouse's hand)* A deal?

Mouse: I could get a lot done in three years.

(Omega appears to consider.)

I'd put the time to good use.

Omega: Like you've put the last seventy years to good use?

Mouse: Don't be cruel.

Omega: Any other bright ideas?

Mouse: Be serious!

(Omega is getting bored.)

Pity me.

Omega: *(scathingly)* Pity you! Whatever next!

Mouse: Give me another chance.

Omega: Nah!

Mouse: It couldn't do any harm for you to look the other way for a year or two.

Omega: Nope.

Mouse: I'd reform.

Omega: A likely story.

Mouse: Do some good in the world.

Omega: *(very sceptically)* Oh?

Mouse: … give all my money to the poor, for example.

Omega: You don't have any money.

Mouse: … contribute to my country's wellbeing.

Omega: The best contribution you can make right now is to EXPIRE and leave some space for the next generation.

Mouse: … but I want to ACHIEVE something.

Omega: You should have thought of that sooner.

Mouse: I've been busy!

Omega: Lazy.

Mouse: Hey, that's not fair …

Omega: OK, thoughtless. You like that better?

Mouse: *(sulkily)* No, I don't.

Omega: Look on the bright side. No one's saying you've done much good in the world, but then again you haven't done much harm either, or not more than usual. Hard to calculate. We won't know the final tally til long after you've – which do you prefer, died, passed on, passed over, kicked the bucket, turned up your toes?

Mouse: *(crossly)* I don't like any of them.

Omega: But given you want a last project to keep your mind off things, there's always your son in law.

Mouse: Eh?

Omega: Your son in law. Your daughter's husband. The father of your grandchildren. The guy you quarrel with.

Mouse: The pompous idiot, you mean!

Omega: There's no harm in him.

Mouse: Yes there is. She deserves better.

Omega: That's a matter of opinion.

Mouse: Well, in my opinion, he's a miserable toad and not worthy of her.

Omega: She loves him.

Mouse: Yeah, to spite me.

Omega: Well my advice is to make your peace with the guy.

Mouse: No.

Omega: It's recommended procedure before dying.

Mouse: *(sarcastically)* Along with tidying the house and wearing clean underwear?

Omega: *(piously)* It would be a generous gesture.

Mouse: So would postponing the date of my execution … you know I'd have made a pact with the devil to have that girl happy. That's not too much to ask, is it? No, she has to go her own way – marry the toad *(croaking)*, have a pack of children …

Omega: Come on, you can't still be worrying about her.

Mouse: Yes I can.

Omega: She's nearly forty.

Mouse: What's that got to do with it!

Malik: *(irritably)* ... and now you have to part, the two of you, right?

Mouse: Yes. Without anything being settled.

Malik: Well, settle it then.

Mouse: *(indignantly)* It's not up to me!

Malik: Of course it's up to you.

Mouse: It's her duty to, to—

Malik: To, to?

Mouse: Stop torturing me the way she does. I haven't had a quiet moment since the day she was born.

Malik: It's not HER fault you worry about her.

Mouse: *(knowing he's being unreasonable)* Yes it is. I should have strangled her at birth ...

Malik: Way to go!

Mouse: It would have been easier than this.

Malik: Eh?

Mouse: *(sighing)* ... saying goodbye ... what to say, what not to say? Garrulous old idiot? Stern patriarch?

(Mouse puts his head in his hands in despair and groans.)

Omega: *(to Malik)* Remind me again. A heart problem, you said?

Malik: Yup.

Omega: Prognosis?

Malik: Nothing more they can do. It's just a question of time. He went to his appointment at the hospital a reasonably roly poly sort of mouse, left a skinny, flattened out sort of mouse.

Omega: *(insincerely)* Poor Mouse.

Malik: *(to Mouse who is rocking in despair)* That's enough! Come on, you're wasting time. You

	have a performance to prepare for! *(handing a script to Mouse)* Here's the plot summary.
Mouse:	*(reading)* "In the mind of Mouse a civil war is raging."
Malik:	Go on.
Mouse:	"On the one side, Terror."
Malik:	On the other?
Mouse:	"Calm." *(flicking through the script)* Terror is making most of the big speeches.
Omega:	A proper villain.
Mouse:	Calm, on the other hand—
Omega:	Lazy bitch—
Mouse:	Hardly opens her mouth.
Malik:	*(sternly)* Notwithstanding, Calm is the heroine of the piece and Terror is to get his comeuppance. That's simple enough.
Mouse:	*(acting)* "Terror away!"
Malik:	With feeling.

Mouse: *(trying out different voices)* Terror away! Away! Away! Away! *(then as if trying to coax a child)* Calm, my pet, stop hiding, come out, hold my hand, work your magic ... *(aside to Malik, pointing to Omega)* Never leaves the room these days, not for a moment.

Malik: I know.

Mouse: I'm on permanent alert ... it's very uncomfortable ... I blame the doctor, she should have lied and said it was nothing serious.

Malik: Not when you told her you wanted the truth.

Mouse: Yeah, well, that was before I knew what the truth would feel like ... she couldn't have been wrong, Malik? *(dreaming)* Muddled the notes maybe? She's a young woman, the baby keeps her awake at night, she misreads the test results—

Malik: Doubt it.

Mouse: ... the hope won't die that this is all some stupid mistake. The judge was dozy, I got the wrong sentence, on appeal I'll be freed and get back to my old life ... makes me restless, Malik.

Malik: I know.

Mouse: There are days I feel as good as new—

Omega: *(studying Mouse)* Yeah well, you don't look as good as new, you look old.

(Omega tries to make Mouse stand up straight by putting a knee in his back and pulling back his shoulders so he doesn't appear hunched over.)

Mouse: Ow!

Omega: It's your own fault. You've let yourself go. Well, if you like staring at your feet all day – *(mimicking a penguin)*

Mouse: It's NOT my fault. It's part of the aging process. *(as a litany)* The vertebrae shift—

Malik: The eyes dim—

Mouse: Teeth decay—

Malik: Hair fades—

Omega: *(inspecting Mouse)* Maybe you should stay out of sight.

Mouse: I AM out of sight. I wander the streets invisible. Or if I AM seen I know the seer is mentally putting me on an ice floe and shoving me out to sea ... *(addressing Omega)* Hurry up, goddam you, if you're going to strike, strike! Let's get it over with.

Omega: *(sharpening the scythe)* All in good time.

Mouse: Waiting, waiting, waiting—

Omega: I know, I am a tease.

(Omega swings his scythe in Mouse's direction, Mouse backs away.)

You want me to strike or don't you?

(Mouse moves back again.)

Don't be greedy. You've had seventy years plus. That's not bad.

Mouse: *(angrily)* Yeah, well, I want MORE.

Omega: Come on, you've always known this isn't a "They lived happily ever after" story. Be reasonable. Bow your head—

Mouse: *(interrupting)* And accept the inevitable? Thank you, but no ... how about six months, then I agree to go quietly?

Omega: I don't bargain.

Mouse: Everybody bargains.

Omega: Not Death.

Mouse: *(grumbling under his breath)* Well, I'm not going before Mrs Snodgrass goes.

Omega: You'll go when I say.

Mouse: You ever stop to think what that woman is costing society?

Omega: I am completely uninterested in economics.

Mouse: Well, I can tell you! A fortune!

Omega: *(suddenly very aggressive)* Didn't you hear me? I said I am not interested.

(Mouse cowers back.)

Mouse: *(gibbering)* If you think you're frightening me—

Omega: I don't think I am, I know I am.

Mouse: Yeah, well, I do not like the idea of eternal oblivion.

Malik: There's no need to panic. Play your cards right and the family will remember you now and again. *(sotto voce)* If you're lucky.

Mouse: Yeah, and then they die and I'm a goner for good.

Malik: How about getting yourself buried in the local churchyard! Then for hundreds of years strangers will pass by and read your name on the tombstone and wonder who the hell Mouse, died June the fifth, two thousand and eighteen, was.

Mouse: That's the best you can offer by way of immortality?

Malik: It's better than nothing.

Mouse: *(seriously)* It's pitiful.

Malik: Yes, it is.

(a slight pause)

Mouse: Maybe I misheard and jumped to the wrong conclusion. I thought she said "Prepare to meet thy doom." I could have been wrong.

Malik: Well, you weren't wrong.

Mouse: Maybe this is all a big mistake.

Malik: *(quietly)* No mistake, Mouse.

(Mouse flops into a chair and falls face down on the table, He lies there unmoving, completely defeated.)

Omega: *(counting Mouse out)* One, two, three, that's it, he's out for the count.

Malik: *(to Mouse)* Don't just lie there!

Omega: Four, five, six, he's given up.

Malik: Mouse, on your feet. Now!

Omega: Seven, eight, nine—

(Malik pulls Mouse up. Mouse gets up and paces in a very agitated way.)

Mouse: I've made my decision, they're not to come, Malik!

Malik: Who's not to come?

Mouse: The family, of course! What for? To poke their noses into my business and sniff around the house looking for objects of value they've got their eye on …

Malik: They won't be looking for objects of value, you old fool—

Mouse: Yes, they will.

Malik: *(barely restraining himself)* Because there aren't any! And even if there were they wouldn't like them, they're a different generation.

Mouse: *(mulishly)* I don't want them here.

Malik: Oh, why not? … … Come on, spit it out!

Mouse: *(low voice)* Because I might let them down.

Malik: *(seriously)* Well, you mustn't.

Mouse: I don't trust myself, Malik.

Malik: *(quietly)* Who does!

Mouse: What if they come, we quarrel and everything goes wrong?

Malik: *(seriously)* It can't go wrong.

Mouse: It's too risky.

Malik: They HAVE to come.

Mouse: *(to himself, in a low voice)* Why? To see how weak I am? To walk through the door and not to recognize me?

Malik: *(falsely dramatic)* A knock on the portal. Mouse answers. They fall back in horror. "Who is this small, misshapen creature?" they cry … or maybe they laugh …

Mouse: *(strutting)* I was somebody once, eh Malik? Big Man Mouse! *(then despairing)* It's true, I'm hunched now, misshapen. It's embarrassing. Drains my confidence. On top of that there's not being able to get out of my chair, tripping, or worst case scenario, falling over – plus in cold weather the drip on the end of my nose—

Omega: Don't you worry, Mousie, it won't be for long, your heart's going to go pop at any moment.

(Mouse faints at this.)

Oops. Something I said?

(Malik and Omega help Mouse up. Mouse is very unsteady.)

Malik: You fainted! In front of the enemy.

Mouse: He threatened me!

Malik: That's no excuse.

Mouse: It was a moment of panic.

Malik: It was disgraceful.

Mouse: *(still excusing himself)* You heard him. He said my heart would go POP. I saw blood everywhere, Malik.

Malik: Nonsense.

Mouse: Then a ravaged bleeding corpse lying in the dust.

Malik: This isn't a Western.

Mouse: *(with pathos)* Mutilated. Alone … remember a time when we didn't think about dying, Malik?

Malik: I do.

Mouse: *(nostalgically)* What innocents we were!

Omega: *(sotto voce)* What fools!

Mouse: Wandering Paradise, no thought for the future.

Malik: *(very tartly)* It was never Paradise.

(Malik snaps his fingers in front of Mouse to bring him back from his dream.)

(like a stage director) Come on, back to work. There's a difficult scene coming up. Sorry, Mouse, there's no easy way to say this, but you're dying, or will be soon and the family does have to visit and of course it may be awkward. The last thing we want is for old grudges to resurface! The situation needs a firm hand. Yours! You will be leading the negotiations. And it's your responsibility to see that there are no serious disagreements. This is a meeting that HAS to end well. You'll be in charge—

Omega: *(sotto voce)* I'll be in charge—

Malik: *(to Mouse)* You hear that? Boasting as usual. But – listen carefully – from now on, you have new obligations. You're not to let Omega rile you. Or take control. Or confuse you. *(waving* *the ms)* It's all in the script. You stand firm. For the family's sake.

Mouse: Standing firm!

(Mouse stands firm. Omega makes horrible voodoo noises and gestures. Mouse, by a great effort of will stands firm. Omega moves away sulking. Mouse is shaky. He sits down and groans.)

Malik: What's the problem? That was good!

Mouse: My knees are wobbly.

Malik: *(crossly)* You're trembling!

Mouse: *(stubbornly)* Yeah, well, he frightens me. *(shouting at Omega)* Bully!

Omega: You be careful, Mousie. I can make things very tough for you.

Mouse: *(to Malik)* You hear that? He's threatening me again.

Omega: You bet I am! Think of all the tricks I have up my sleeve. I can deprive you of speech, paralyse you, blind you – there's no end to the mischief I can get up to.

Mouse: *(half bowing)* Mighty Omega.

Omega: That's better.

Mouse: Great Seigneur.

(Omega moves away.)

(to Malik, whispering) Nearly had his clammy hand on me.

Malik: I saw.

Mouse: … you figure if I'm VERY polite he might …

Malik: Reconsider? Forget about you? Take Mrs S instead? No.

Mouse: My problem is, despite all the odds, I still hope, Malik. I can't seem to help myself. *(dreaming)* For example, the forecast this week is for sunny spells. Did you hear that? Sunny spells mean moments of magic as the world brightens … I can't see myself missing them.

(Omega makes a noise with his scythe.)

Malik: *(coldly to Mouse)* You have to let go.

Mouse: I'm trying to.

Malik: No you're not. You're harping on about everything you can't see yourself missing. It's unbearable. This is the final test, Mouse, and so far you're failing miserably.

Mouse: *(standing upright, fists at the ready)* OK, here goes, hero mode. *(to Omega)* Do what you like with me, deprive me of speech, paralyse me, see if I care … *(breaking down)* no, don't, don't, no paralysis, no dementia, I beg of you.

(Omega stalks Mouse like a cat. Mouse squeaks and tries to get away.)

Omega: *(playfully)* I'm after you.

Mouse: Mind your manners. I'm a sick old man, I DEMAND respect.

Omega: Mouse, my friend, your demanding days are over.

Mouse: *(pompously)* Here I am, a pillar of society—

Omega: But a very foolish pillar! Haven't you noticed yet that society is changing, moving on, that it doesn't have time for you? The new ideas and the new technology are leaving you behind.

You can't manage on your own anymore, you need a guide. You're a hanger on now, not a player. Hangers on are troublesome, wheedling creatures – that's where I come in – I tidy up, clear out the old wood, make way for new growth.

(Mouse makes as though to spit at Omega. Malik places himself between Omega and Mouse.)

Malik: Cool it, both of you!

(Omega exhales heavily over Mouse.)

Mouse: *(reeling back from the stink of Omega's breath)* He stinks. He's insufferable! It's no wonder I fainted.

Malik: What did I say back there? No …?

Mouse: *(hanging his head)* No excuses.

(a short pause)

The family come through the door, what will they see, Malik? A small, shrunken—

Omega: *(sotto voce)* Pathetic—

Mouse: Object of pity …

Malik: Maybe, or maybe they'll see a tyrant overthrown to make way for their brave new world?

Mouse: *(drily)* A gang of youngsters with no experience looking to take MY place!

Malik: A gang of youngsters with new ideas and higher hopes.

Mouse: …and if I live on for another twenty years?

Malik: You'll be sat quietly in a corner, comfortable enough—

Mouse: But with no authority …

Omega: Like I say, a hanger on—

Mouse: A troublesome, wheedling creature—

Malik: *(gently)* Hush.

(a slight pause)

Omega: *(looking at his watch)* Dear me, there's another half hour gone. Time does fly when you're enjoying yourself.

Mouse: I'm not enjoying myself.

Omega: I am. I have a scaredy, quarrelsome little fool of a mouse to keep me amused.

Mouse: *(with his hands over his ears, to Malik)* Shut him up, Malik.

Malik: YOU shut him up.

Mouse: He's picking on me.

Malik: *(impatiently)* Don't show him you're scared then.

Mouse: *(stuttering)* No .. no.. not sca ... sca –scare ...

Malik: Scared!

Mouse: *(in a very small voice)* Scared! Very scared!

Malik: NOT scared! Why do I bother!

Mouse: Not scared. *(to Omega)* Not scared. Not scared.

Omega: Liar.

Malik: *(exasperated)* Stop! Both of you!

(Omega sticks his tongue out at Mouse, Mouse makes a face at Omega.)

(to Mouse) Now, imagine yourself being led in chains through the streets of Rome, the captive of an all powerful Caesar, with the eyes of the world upon you, you're not going to snivel are you? Or stutter when spoken to? Or faint? You're going to hold your head up and confront your executioner with calm!

Mouse: But Malik, I'm not being led in chains through the streets of Rome. Quite the contrary—

(Omega is honing and whistling.)

(of Omega) He's tortures me, Malik.

Malik: Of course he does, that's his job.

Mouse: Inching closer everyday, winking at me—

Malik: I know.

Mouse: That's weeks I've been under surveillance, day and night, no let up, it's not a life.

Malik: No.

Mouse: No real hope of hope, can't plan, can't dream …

Malik: I know.

Mouse: Please, Malik, make an effort, say something positive.

Malik: *(considers)* No.

Mouse: No comfort? No consolation?

(Malik shrugs.)

Tomorrow I wake up – if I'm lucky – get out of bed, eat my breakfast – if I've got the appetite for it – then what? Stare at Omega for the next sixteen hours until it's time to go to bed again?

Malik: *(irritated)* Go dancing! Find a partner!

Mouse: Not possible! The gods have turned me to stone.

(Malik starts to do a little tap dance, Mouse slowly joins in. They tap dance together, Mouse is happy. Mouse stops suddenly.)

Are you crazy! I can't enjoy myself!

Malik: Why not?

Mouse: Because I'm a man condemned, remember! You heard the sentence. Prison and execution await.

Omega: *(crooning sentimentally)* Imagine Death is like sleep—

Mouse: *(crossly)* It's nothing like sleep because I WON'T WAKE UP. *(tossing Omega a coin)* Here, buzz off, go and buy yourself a lollipop.

Omega: *(virtuously)* I don't take bribes.

Mouse: Everyone takes bribes.

Omega: Not Death.

(A frightened pause and then Mouse shows courage.)

Mouse: *(grandiosely)* I've changed my mind. I AM IMMORTAL.

Malik: No, you're not.

Mouse: Well, today I feel immortal.

Malik: Feeling immortal is a trick nature plays on us particularly when we're young. You're an old bag of bones. That's what you are.

Mouse: *(stubbornly)* An immortal old bag of bones.

Malik: Don't be so stubborn.

Mouse: I have plans, projects—

Malik: And a weak heart!

Mouse: I might live for another twenty years, into serene old age.

Malik: Old age is not serene, it's cruel, a fight with one hand tied behind your back and no chance of winning.

Omega: With me the victor!

Malik: *(seriously)* And for each and every one of us a fight of Biblical proportions.

(Mouse timidly gives Omega a little push. Omega is angry and pushes Mouse to the ground and kicks at him. Malik helps him up.)

Mouse: *(whispering)* Got a very nasty temper.

Malik: I told you.

Mouse: *(whispering)* Never going to listen on the subject of extra time?

Malik: No.

Mouse: … but I'll keep on asking. Can't help myself… "Please sir, another twenty four hours." It's in the genes.

Malik: … it's true, you MIGHT live for years …

Mouse: Or die tomorrow.

Malik: Could be easy.

Mouse: Could be hard.

Malik: Ladies, gentlemen, here's our contender, place your bets. *(to Mouse)* Come on, stand up, turn round, let them have a good look at you. *(to the audience)* So what do you say? You sir, a couple of weeks, a month at most? Or you, Madam, you figure he's going to beat the odds and live til he's ninety, miracles can happen after all? Will it be quick or will it be slow? a sprint to his death or a marathon?

Mouse: *(not listening)* … why can't we start over?

Malik: Rewrite the script—

Mouse: Begin again—

Malik: Have a second chance—

Mouse: Be what we dreamed of being.

Omega: *(impatiently)* Begin again! Have a second chance! I'm not listening to this claptrap.

(Omega hones his scythe.)

Mouse: I wish he'd stop doing that.

Malik: It's a test.

Mouse: I know.

Malik: Part of the ritual.

Mouse: SSSS, it keeps me awake at night.

Malik: It's meant to.

Mouse: *(low voice)* Then he stands over my bed, looking down at me, and I can't think straight, the room spins, I lose my bearings …

Malik: *(massaging Mouse's shoulders)* Remember the watchword?

Mouse: *(shaking his fist at Omega)* Calm? *(paranoid)* Calm! With Omega glaring at me!

Malik: Yeah, well, see it from his point of view, you're seventy plus, your health is bad, your memory is deteriorating in short you're no longer fit for purpose. I don't think it's personal.

Mouse: "A horse, a horse, my kingdom for a horse!"

Malik: You don't have a kingdom.

(Omega taps Mouse on the shoulder, Mouse is startled.)

Mouse: My hour has come!

Omega: *(rubbing his hands and smiling)* Very true. The party's over. Time to take your bow, old man.

(Malik is watching Omega who is testing the blade of the scythe.)

Malik: Looks like he's getting ready for action.

Mouse: *(to Omega, gesturing with his thumb)* Right next door, guv. Number thirty five. Mrs Snodgrass is the name. She'll be glad to see you.

Malik: Please, you're embarrassing me.

Mouse: *(passionately)* I don't care. I want to LIVE, Malik. She doesn't.

(Omega comes closer to Mouse.)

(to Omega) You're early!

Omega: Not at all. Right on time.

Mouse: I'm not ready.

Omega: And whose fault is that?

Mouse: You'll have to wait.

Omega: Oh I will, will I?

Mouse: I'm going to travel.

Omega: No, you're not.

Mouse: *(forcefully)* Here's my itinerary. I'm seeing everything, from the Arctic circle to the Saharan deserts – it'll take years.

Malik: But you don't like the cold. Or the heat.

Mouse: I like EVERYTHING. Everything ... the cold, the heat, the wild, the domestic, the city, the country, every stick, every stone, every tree, every leaf—

Malik: *(apologising to Omega)* Sorry about this.

Omega: Don't worry. It's nothing I haven't heard many, many times before.

Mouse: I won't let go.

Malik: *(whispering crossly)* Hush, you're behaving like a child.

Mouse: I told you! I don't care.

Malik: Well, I do. *(indicating Omega)* Can't you see he's laughing at you.

Omega: *(putting his face right up to Mouse's)* Ho, ho, ho, little Mousie.

(Mouse kicks angrily at Omega.)

Mouse: This is MY house, clear out.

Omega: Fool.

Mouse: You can't just walk in here whenever it suits you—

Omega: Yes I can.

Mouse: *(shouting)* It's not polite! Shoo, go away, eff off—

Malik: Stop quarreling with him, it only makes things worse.

Mouse: I can smell his dirty breath on me!

Malik: We don't have time to waste fighting. There's still urgent business to be taken care of.

Mouse: *(sulkily)* Urgent business? What are you talking about? I don't understand.

Malik: Yes, you do.

(a slight pause)

Mouse: … I suppose you mean you want me to—

Malik: *(somberly)* Face up to the reality? Yes, I do.

Mouse: *(very quickly)* No.

Malik: And play the role that's been given you without grumbling.

(Mouse stands on a stool.)

Mouse: *(declaiming)* Now showing, the one-time-only performance of "The Death of Mouse."

Malik: Written by Mouse.

Mouse: Devised by Mouse.

Malik: Choreographed by Mouse.

(Mouse squeaks.)

And music by Mouse.

Mouse: Your last chance to see Mouse on stage at the height of his powers. *(bowing to the audience and stepping down from his stool, suddenly deflated)* OK, so I've given my last performance, now what?

Malik: You die. The house is sold, your goods and property dispersed—

Mouse: The little world I built, all ravaged ... ... it's hard, Malik.

Malik: Patience, old fellow.

Mouse: Patience!

Malik: OK, a show of patience.

Mouse: *(sternly)* No fuss.

Malik: Correct.

Mouse: ... all those people who die young, how do they do it?

Malik: *(very seriously)* I don't know.

Mouse: The big question is, Malik—

Malik: I know what the question is.

Mouse: *(low tone)* What if I'm tested beyond my strength?

Malik: Ah.

Mouse: ... say it's a long, drawn out, painful process ... will I falter, crack up, disgrace myself?

(Malik shrugs.)

(low voice) lose my identity?

Malik: *(coldly)* We don't know and there's no point guessing.

Mouse: ... I remember Mrs Snodgrass in her prime! She was a smart, elegant woman, she had everything ... now look at her! That's fifteen years she's taken of it, Malik.

Malik: Yup.

Mouse: And it's not over yet.

Malik: No.

Mouse: (*slowly*) What that woman has suffered.

(*a slight pause*)

(*remembering*) "Mouse" says the doctor, "your time's running out." Well, not those words exactly but that was the gist of it. I'm in shock. I tremble. I try to hide it. I do not succeed. Then, "Enjoy the summer" says she, "it may be your last." Again, not her exact words. I lean forward, I have a million questions to ask her … I don't ask any of them. I open my mouth to object … nothing! Imagine! I enter her office at ten forty five with a few chest pains, by eleven o'clock I'm on death row. Justice has been perverted. I walk home, I don't hear the traffic, I open the front door, and who do I find sitting in my chair?

Omega: I'm not saying I've never nodded to the fellow before, but it's the first time he's invited himself to live with me. Moved in lock, stock and barrel. He WATCHES me, Malik.

(*Mouse, very agitated, paces up and down in front of Omega who sits like a spectator watching a tennis match.*)

See! It's horrible.

Malik: Ignore him!

Mouse: Don't be stupid!

Malik: *(irritably)* And stop pacing.

Mouse: Hmm?

Malik: You're fidgeting.

Mouse: It's the waiting ... it's ... awful ... *(can't find the word)*

Malik: I know.

Mouse: And alone.

Malik: Yes.

Mouse: Never knowing when the blow is going to fall. Today, tomorrow ... I can't sit still, I can't focus, food has no taste ... admit it, he ruins everything.

Malik: Yeah, well, there's no point sulking.

Mouse: I am not sulking, I'm—

Omega: Looks like sulking to me.

Mouse: *(half to himself)* I'm frightened.

Omega: *(mockingly)* No!

Mouse: *(to himself)* ... I should have put out my hand to her ...

Malik: Yup.

Mouse: But I didn't.

Malik: Ah, time now for, "Mouse's regrets." Small regrets, big ones, popular ones, rare ones, family regrets, career regrets, Mouse adds to his stock year on year. You want to talk regrets, Mouse is your man, a real pro, knows everything there is to know on the subject.

Mouse: *(as though giving a lecture, addressing his audience.)* My speciality? The family regret. Messing up your ties with first your parents and then your children. It's so easy. Anyone can do it. Just step right up and try your luck. A moment of carelessness, of irritation and there's another relationship out the window. And good riddance. " They got what they deserved the bastards." But in the final years – we're lonely now – vulnerable, we recognize what we've thrown away— a regret forms, starts small, grows, expands—

(Malik and Omega are heckling.)

Malik: Rubbish.

Omega: Nonsense.

Malik: Sit down, you old bore.

Omega: Nothing original. Like I say I've heard it all a million times before.

(Mouse is coming over to batter them both, but stumbles. Malik offers Mouse his walking stick.)

Malik: If you can't walk without falling over, USE YOUR STICK.

Mouse: No.

Malik: Before I hit you over the head with it.

Mouse: *(taking the stick crossly)* OK, OK.

Malik: Why can't you admit you need it?

Mouse: *(fantasizing, flambouyantly)* Because I'm young, strong, capable. And in my day an athlete! I have a reputation to maintain.

Malik: *(quietly)* You were never an athlete.

Mouse: I won the hundred yard sprint.

Malik: When you were eight.

Mouse: *(dreaming)* I remember it like it was yesterday. The applause, people clapping, the glow of victory, the look on my father's face … wonderful stuff … nothing to beat it … … it should all have been like that day …

Malik: … he wasn't a bad man.

Mouse: But a hard man to please. "One goal achieved, son, look for the next, excel, never let up" on and on … I'll never make sense of it.

Malik: You can't still be angry with him.

Mouse: Yes I can. There's no law against it.

Malik: Well, my advice is to make your peace with whoever done you wrong, and now, before it's too late.

Mouse: *(grumbling)* But it HURTS to let go a grudge, Malik.

Malik: OK, die angry!

Mouse: *(sadly)* I don't want to die angry. *(angrily)* I don't want to die!

(Mouse shakes a fist at Omega. Omega puts an arm around Mouse.)

Omega: That's my boy.

(Mouse trembles with fright at contact with Omega.)

Malik: Now what's wrong? You're as white as a sheet.

Mouse: It's an allergic reaction. *(to Omega)* If you'd stand further off I could catch my breath.

Omega: *(beating his chest)* I am Omega, lord of all, grand destroyer of civilisations, I stand where I like.

(Malik pulls Mouse away from Omega.)

Malik: *(angrily)* Wipe your nose.

(Mouse wipes his nose on his sleeve.)

Not on your sleeve. *(sniffing)* You peed yourself!

Mouse: *(looking down to make sure)* ... no, I didn't ... but I might have, oh, oh, oh ...

Omega:	*(strutting up and down)* Who's the king of the castle!
	(Mouse and Malik hide behind the sofa.)
	Come out.
Mouse:	*(in unison)* We're not playing.
Malik:	*(in unison)* We're not playing.
	(Omega hides in the shadows. Malik looks out from behind the sofa tentatively.)
	OK, all clear.
Mouse:	He's gone?
Malik:	For the moment.
	(Mouse comes out from behind the sofa and dusts himself off.)
Omega:	*(emerging from the shadows)* Peek a boo!
	(Malik and Mouse both jump.)
Mouse:	*(tearfully)* You said he'd gone.
Malik:	I said for the moment.

Mouse: *(agitated)* You tricked me.

(Mouse is slinking behind the sofa again, Omega pulls him away.)

Omega: There's no point hiding. I have a nose like a truffle hound. Come on out and face your future like a man.

(Mouse comes out trembling.)

You've been drinking!

Mouse: Only to calm my nerves before the battle, my lord.

Malik: *(standing Mouse as straight as possible)* Make an effort, can't you! Put your shoulders back! Stand straight!

(Mouse stands as upright as possible, but looks shrunken and miserable. Malik is trying to make Mouse look less hunched and pathetic.)

If you want to do right by your family and friends then show them a brave face.

(a slight pause)

Mouse: I do want to, Malik, but it's difficult with Omega breathing down my neck.

Malik: Well, you can't let them you see you like this.

Mouse: I know.

Malik: You have a duty of care.

Mouse: I know.

Malik: You owe it to them to put on a good show.

Mouse: I know! I've got it! OK? I just can't DO it!

Malik: You're an actor, aren't you? Act!

Mouse: I'm trying to.

Malik: *(indicating a space)* This is your stage here, you have full license to present yourself in any guise you want. So you learn your lines, you take a deep breath and when the time comes, you FOOL them.

Mouse: *(quietly to himself)* I fool them.

Malik: Imagine if they were here at the door right now, what would they see? Mr Gloomy in person. "Mr Gloomy" they'd ask as they entered. "How are you doing?" *(as Mouse, cheerless and groaning)* "Oh, you know, could be better."

Mouse: *(cheerless, gloomy, introducing Omega to the family)* "Meet my new best friend."

Omega: *(stepping forward and bowing)* "Omega. At your service."

Mouse: *(cheerless)* "Fellow's come to live with me. *(paranoid, whispering)* I don't like him, he abuses me ... but don't say anything to bother him ... he can be very spiteful ..."

Malik: *(groaning)* "Boo hoo."

Mouse: *(wailing miserably)* "Oh, oh, oh."

Malik: *(briskly, as himself)* Mouse, who's the heroine of this piece? ... come on, don't play dumb, I know you know the answer.

Mouse: *(grumpily)* Calm.

Malik: That's right, Calm. SHE's your new best friend. You call on her.

Mouse: Come Calm, my dear, show your pretty little face. *(stretching out his hand to an imaginary* *figure)* I see her, I do, but so far off ... *(to Malik)* I move closer, she moves away. *(very agitated, addressing the figure)* She teases me worse than Omega.

Malik: Please! What did the doctor say! No excitement!

Mouse: She said. "You're going to die soon. But don't get excited about it." That was her contribution.

Malik: That is NOT what she said.

Mouse: Then she smiled sweetly and ushered me out.

Malik: She did not smile.

Mouse: Leaving not one glimmer of hope.

Malik: Mouse—

Mouse: The woman was pitiless.

Malik: *(twiddling his thumbs waiting for Mouse to calm down)* Mouse!

Mouse: Told me to get my affairs sorted. *(looking around despairingly)* How? There's nowhere to start. It's hopeless.

(Mouse starts to tidy in an agitated way.)

Omega: *(put out)* Hey, stop that! You concentrate on ME, old man. *(poking Mouse with the handle of his scythe)*

(no reply.)

Do you hear?

Mouse: Of course I hear. I'm not deaf.

(Omega is circling Mouse like a boxer, fists up, throwing punches.)

Omega: So come on, I want some fun

(Mouse reels, taking punishment.)

Move your feet, stay upright, dodge the punches, make me laugh—

(Mouse stumbles and collapses onto the sofa. Omega laughs.)

If you could see yourself!

Mouse: *(seriously)* I do see myself.

(Mouse tries to get up from the sofa but Omega pushes him back down.)

Omega: (sitting down beside Mouse) Well, isn't this cosy!

(Mouse tries again to move away.)

No, you stay right here.

Mouse: … do me one favour, Omega, make it quick … promise me!

Omega: *(coldly)* I never make promises.

Mouse: *(to himself)* It MUST be quick.

Omega: *(very firmly)* Stop whinging. You'll take what comes, like everybody else!

Mouse: … it COULD be quick …

Omega: *(teasing)* It's possible. We'll have to wait and see what mood I'm in at the time.

(a pause, Mouse turns to look very directly at Omega)

Mouse: *(addressing Omega, seriously)* I'm not your plaything you know, to do as you like with.

Omega: Aren't you?

Mouse: No ... yes ... no ...

Omega: Come on, you've always known what was ahead of you. I haven't hidden myself out of sight for the last seventy years or ever kidded you it was going to be easy. Our eyes have met across a crowded room on many occasions. It's been your decision to blank me out, to pretend I didn't exist, to tell yourself there'd be no final rendez-vous.

Mouse: ... I wasn't expecting you so soon.

Omega: More fool you.

Mouse: You walk in here like you own the place—

Omega: And serve you with an eviction order? Yup.

Mouse: With the intention of silencing me for ever!

Omega: That's the plan!

Mouse: ... *(to himself)* I'd give anything for a second chance.

Omega: Yeah, well, there are no second chances, not when I've made up my mind.

Mouse: ... *(half to himself)* but I'd change ...

Omega: *(honing his scythe)* Feel that blade! That is a blade that is ready for action NOW!

Mouse: *(anxious)* Malik!

Malik: Now what?

Mouse: He's threatening me again. DO something.

Malik: Do something yourself.

Mouse: I can't. I'm too—

Malik: Hysterical?

Mouse: *(pulling himself together)* Not at all. Cool as a cucumber. *(despairing again)* ... he said "feel the blade."

Malik: One of his little jokes.

Mouse: He was serious.

Malik: I know.

Mouse: It's too soon. I have arrangements to make.

Malik: Yes, you do, choosing your coffin, for example, paying for it, organizing the

	service, selecting the flowers, buying your outfit.
Mouse:	*(confused)* My outfit?
Malik:	Say you're laid out in a funeral parlour – or maybe chez toi – exposed to public view, you'll need to be wearing something decent. What do you fancy? Business suit? Leisure clothes? Top hat and tails?
Mouse:	Are you crazy!
Malik:	Or will you be wanting the coffin closed?
Mouse:	*(confused)* Eh?
Malik:	The coffin! Do – you – want – it – open – or – closed!
Mouse:	*(indignantly)* I don't want to think about things like that.
Malik:	Pine? Oak? Eco friendly? Plain interior or elegant satin lining? You intend to be mummifed or left au nature?
Mouse:	You're teasing. You're no better than Omega. It's cruel. I don't have the stomach for it. Leave me alone.

(Malik moves away.)

Don't go.

(a slight pause)

… I'm tired, Malik.

Malik: One last push, old fellow.

Mouse: Look at me. I'm a joke. Half blind, partially deaf, my legs are weak … how did I get to be like this?

Malik: It's been seventy five, long, hard years.

Mouse: … the old guard are dying off.

Malik: Yup.

Mouse: Makes it lonely.

Malik: Yup.

Mouse: … you'd think I'd be glad to be going … but I'm not.

Malik: No.

Mouse: … I'd stay if I could.

Omega: *(sotto voce)* But you can't.

Mouse: *(in a reverie)* I'd start again ... make all the changes I've always been dreaming of ... *(breaks off)* but I won't, will I? ... it's too late ... and Omega's right, I'm old, I don't fit in anymore, I'm an exile, a foreigner in my own country ... *(low voice)* ... if my conscience was clearer, would it be easier?

Malik: *(shortly)* I don't know.

Mouse: If I'd done more?

(Malik shrugs.)

... or been happier?

Malik: You WERE happy. From time to time.

Mouse: Yes ... a rough and ready sort of happiness – but it's all rough and ready, from the start to the finish, from day one to the last day ... always those little pin- pricks of discontent, or great stab wounds some of them – a sharp word here, a betrayal there ... sickness, loneliness ... *(to Omega)* And much of it YOUR fault. Threatening people, taking wives from husbands, daughters from mothers, friend from friend, whadda you care what misery you cause? Sniffing around for your next victim, sticking your snout into everybody's business, *(changing tone)* ... I won't be reconciled to how shabby it all is, how many compromises have to be made, how many hopes given up, how many disappointments endured – or not endured – how many temptations there are to be resisted, how much pain to be suffered – or inflicted – the petty feuds, the petty grievances, what's left? A happiness with cracks all through it, without value—

Omega: *(yawning)* Aaaamen!

(Omega makes a show of being asleep.)

Mouse: He's not really asleep.

Malik: I know.

Mouse: He never sleeps.

Malik: I know.

Mouse: What age would you say I was, fifty, sixty, when Omega first started putting his nose around the door? Not that I paid much attention. Another five years and he'd taken to camping in the front room for the odd night or two. I didn't like it but I couldn't kick him out. A few years after that and he's following me around like a faithful old dog who won't let me out of his sight. Where ever I go he goes, comes in the car with me, sits on my bed at night, just loves my company and has to be close. There's no getting rid of him.

(Omega does a little bow in acknowledgement.)

And to think we had everything once. Youth, high hopes—

Malik: A dream, a future –

Mouse: *(pointing to Omega)* And no sign of HIM anywhere.

Omega: You have to laugh.

(Mouse turns on Omega and tries to push him over, Omega easily forces Mouse down.)

(sorcerer) On your knees, you old fool! Beg for mercy!

(Mouse is about to go on his knees but Malik prevents him.)

Malik: Can't you remember for one minute what we're trying to do here? To …? To …?

Mouse: … die with dignity?

Malik: Exactly. Kneeling at Omega's feet is not the answer.

Mouse: … you're right.

(Mouse tries to bow obsequiously to Omega, but Malik prevents him.)

Malik: *(sternly)* And neither is bowing! Mouse, this all wrong! We're not getting anywhere. Fetch me the script. It's the script that's faulty. Give me the last few pages, the ending and let's see what we've got here.

(Mouse fetches the script and they study it. They mutter over it while reading with their backs turned on Omega.)

Hum, pain, misery, despair, this is grim stuff, Mouse.

Mouse: I know.

Malik: And in Omega's handwriting. Worse than anything we imagined. It can't be allowed.

Mouse: That's all very well, but –

Malik: You have to rewrite it!

Mouse: Eh?

Malik: Rewrite, revise it!

Mouse: Me!

Malik: Of course you! Who else is there! You're our only hope! *(handing a pen to Mouse)* Get busy! Now! We don't have much time. You tear this ending up and give us another. Hurry!

(Mouse hesitantly starts making changes in the script.)

Omega: *(very suspicious)* What are you doing? What are you up to?

Malik: None of your business.

Omega: Everything is my business.

Malik: *(angrily)* No, it's not.

Omega: *(cold and frightening)* Don't you contradict me!

Malik: *(waving the ms)* Yeah, well, we don't like the end. *(to Mouse)* Go on!

Mouse: So we're changing it.

(They are writing a new ending.)

Omega: You can't change it!

Malik: *(waving the MS)* The last line here reads "Mouse dies in great mental distress." We're betting you wrote that?

Omega: Of course I wrote it.

Malik: Well, Mouse is amending it.

Omega: That's impossible. You're not altering one word!

Malik: *(dictating to Mouse as Mouse writes)* Oh, but I am, you old fool!

Mouse: Oh but I am, you old fool.

Omega: *(beating his chest)* I am all powerful Omega—

Mouse: I know, and I'm one very little mouse, *(writing)* but while I hold a pen in my hand I can still make changes and you can't stop me.

Omega: Don't be impertinent.

(Omega looks at the MS, is very angry, waves a fist at Mouse.)

Malik: *(aside to Mouse)* Bravo! You're annoying him!

Mouse: I know I am. He doesn't like it.

Malik: Of course he doesn't. Neither do I, but it has to be done.

Mouse: He wants everything arranged HIS way.

Malik: I know what he wants, And he's not getting it.

Mouse: We need to be careful, Malik.

Malik: He's our enemy, Mouse, not our master.

Mouse: … I'm scared …

Malik: Trust me.

Mouse: But Malik—

Malik: Shhhh. It's now or never. This isn't a rehearsal, this is the performance. Make the most of it, you won't get a second chance. Stand your ground. Don't let him humiliate you.

(Omega holds Mouse by the arm and is pushing him back.)

Mouse: *(quietly)* You're hurting me.

Omega: *(coldly)* And I'll hurt you more.

Mouse: I know.

Omega: Bow your head, Mousie.

(Mouse very slowly stands as upright as possible and looks Omega full in the face.)

Mouse: No.

Omega: You scum! Where are your manners!

(Mouse does not move. Omega pushes Mouse violently so that he half falls.)

There! How do you like that!

(Malik starts to help Mouse to his feet.)

I'd stay where you are if I was you.

Mouse: But you're not me.

(Mouse wobbles, Malik helps Mouse to stand.)

Omega: *(very angry)* Say you're sorry!

Mouse: Sorry for what?

Omega: Disrespecting me!

Mouse: Oh, that!

Omega: And bow your head!

Mouse: No.

Omega: *(disconcerted)* Well, at least apologise!

Mouse: No.

Omega: *(childishly)* Come on, that's not asking much—

(Malik takes Omega by the ear and leads him to the side of the stage. Mouse is very still.)

(wriggling and angry and childish) Don't be rude. This is MY game. MY rules. It's your job to do as you're told. C'm on, bleat, whimper, make a fool of yourself, I'm running out of patience here.

Malik: *(whispering to Mouse)* I think he's going to have a tantrum!

Mouse: *(whispering)* I know. You have to laugh.

Malik: *(joining in)* to laugh.

(Omega has a tantrum. Neither Malik or Mouse pay any attention.)

Omega: *(begging)* Please, don't be petty. Behave! Play properly! Kneel! Submit!

Mouse: Things change, Omega.

Omega: Yeah, well, you can't just walk away. We're not done here.

Mouse: I'm tired. The end is coming. I have things on my mind.

Omega: *(sulkily, like a child)* Yeah, well, you are not quitting. Not til I say! *(stamping foot)* I'm bored. I need someone to frighten!

Mouse: Well, find someone else.

Omega: Mousie!

(Mouse won't reply, Omega dances in front of him trying to get his attention)

	Sweet Mouse! *(bowing slightly)* Be a good Mouse. Humour me, act the victim, do plead, beg, resist ... I'm asking nicely.
Mouse:	*(considering)* ... um ... ... no ... pe.
Omega:	*(indignantly)* No? No? Mutiny in the ranks! A hundred lashes! ... be nice, old friend ... do show me how wretched you are!
Mouse:	*(quietly)* No.
Omega:	*(childishly)* That's mean. It's not fair.
Mouse:	Stop whinging. *(half smiling)*
Omega:	*(sulkily)* Well, YOU're no fun any more! *(grumpily)* I suppose your heart is bothering you?
	(no reply)
	You can't get your breath?
	(no reply)
	Answer me!
Mouse:	*(half smiling)* My heart is bothering me and I can't get my breath.

Omega: This is serious, Mouse.

Mouse: I know. It's very serious.

Omega: ... *(wheedling)* just one more game?

Mouse: *(quietly)* No.

(Mouse is arranging things tidily.)

Omega: *(shouting)* But Mouse—

Mouse: Lower your voice, I'm busy.

Omega: *(trying to bargain, wheedling)* Come on, bow your head and I'll give you another twenty four hours—

Mouse: Quiet! *(looking around then muttering to himself)* ... will they know how I loved them? ... forgive me ...

(Omega raises the scythe.)

Malik: *(gently)* Mouse.

Mouse: ... it was ignorance ...

Malik: Mouse, his arm is raised.

Mouse: I know

Omega: This is it.

Mouse: I know …

Omega: You're going to die, Mouse. The trap is set.

Mouse: Yes …

Omega: It never fails.

Mouse: No.

Omega: It breaks your back, Mousie.

Mouse: *(with real dignity)* Mister Mouse to you!

Omega: Oh, Mister Mouse now, is it.

Mouse: *(smiling a little)* Mister Mouse, Sir!

Omega: Oh, Mister Mouse, Sir!

Mouse: That's right!

Omega: *(serious and respectful)* Everything in order?

Mouse: *(half smiling, rueful)* No.

Omega: … house tidy? Affairs in order? Fences mended?

Mouse: (half smiling, rueful) … no …

Omega: But you're ready?

Mouse: Yes, I'm ready.

Omega: Good. Just in time.

(They stand facing one another. Omega grasps his scythe. Mouse stands as upright as possible. He is composed. He looks straight at Omega. The curtain comes down as Omega raises his scythe to strike.)